TREE HOUSE
Coloring Book

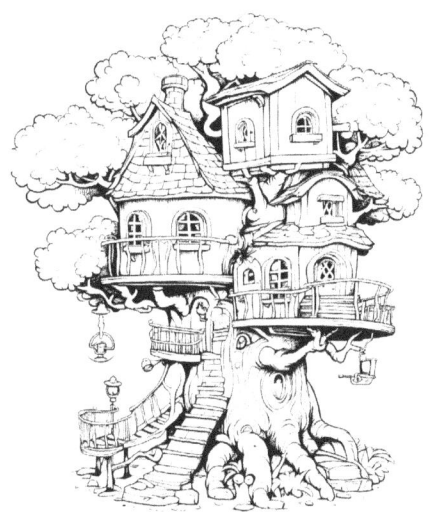

Step into the magical world of tree houses with this delightful coloring book! Featuring 50 unique single-sided coloring pages of intricate illustrations of imaginative tree houses, Whether you're an experienced artist or just want to chill out, these designs are perfect for relaxation and stress relief. Let your imagination run wild as you bring these adorable tree houses to life with colors of your choice. Order your copy today and embark on a painting adventure in the treetops.

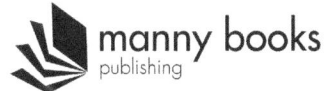

manny books
publishing

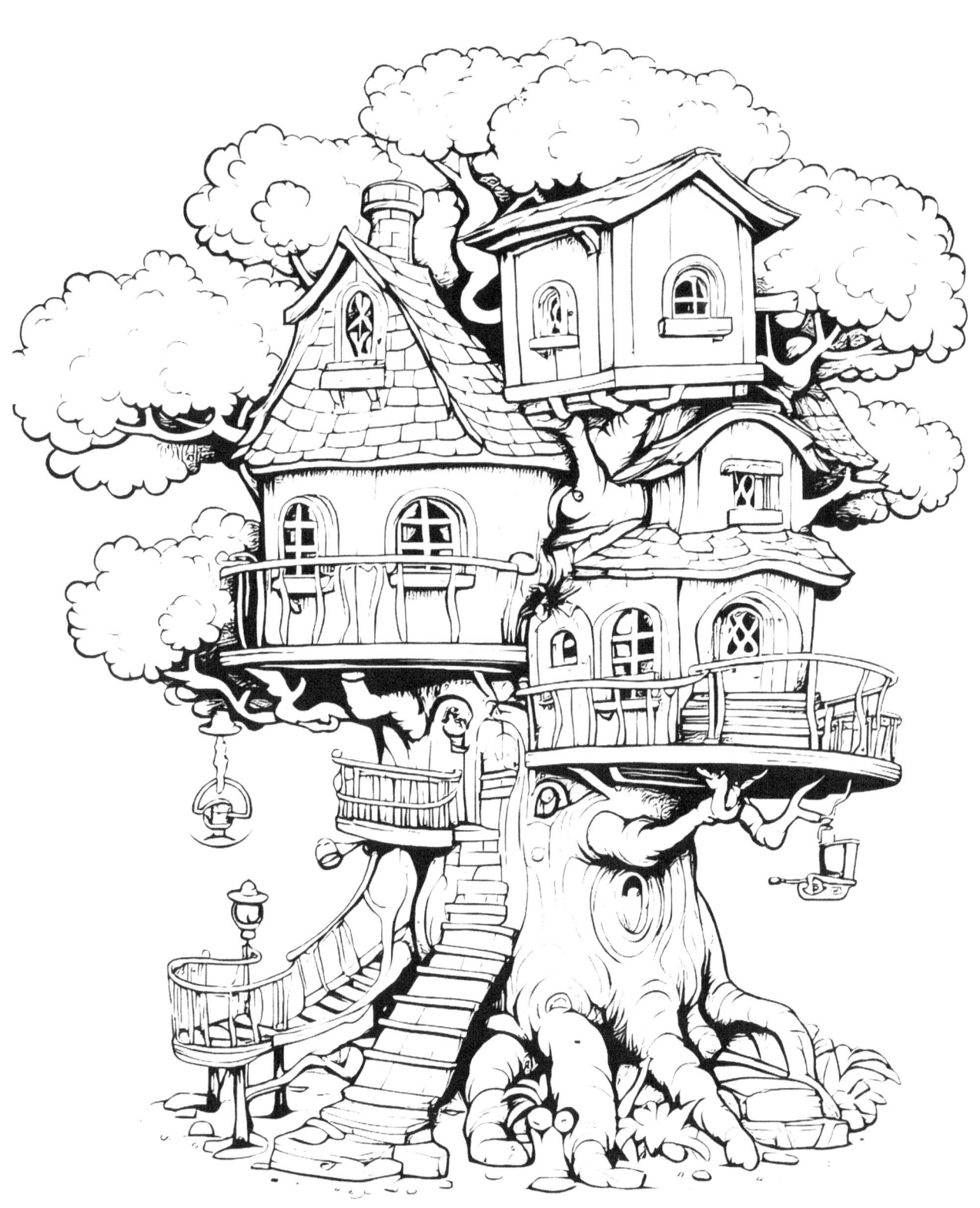

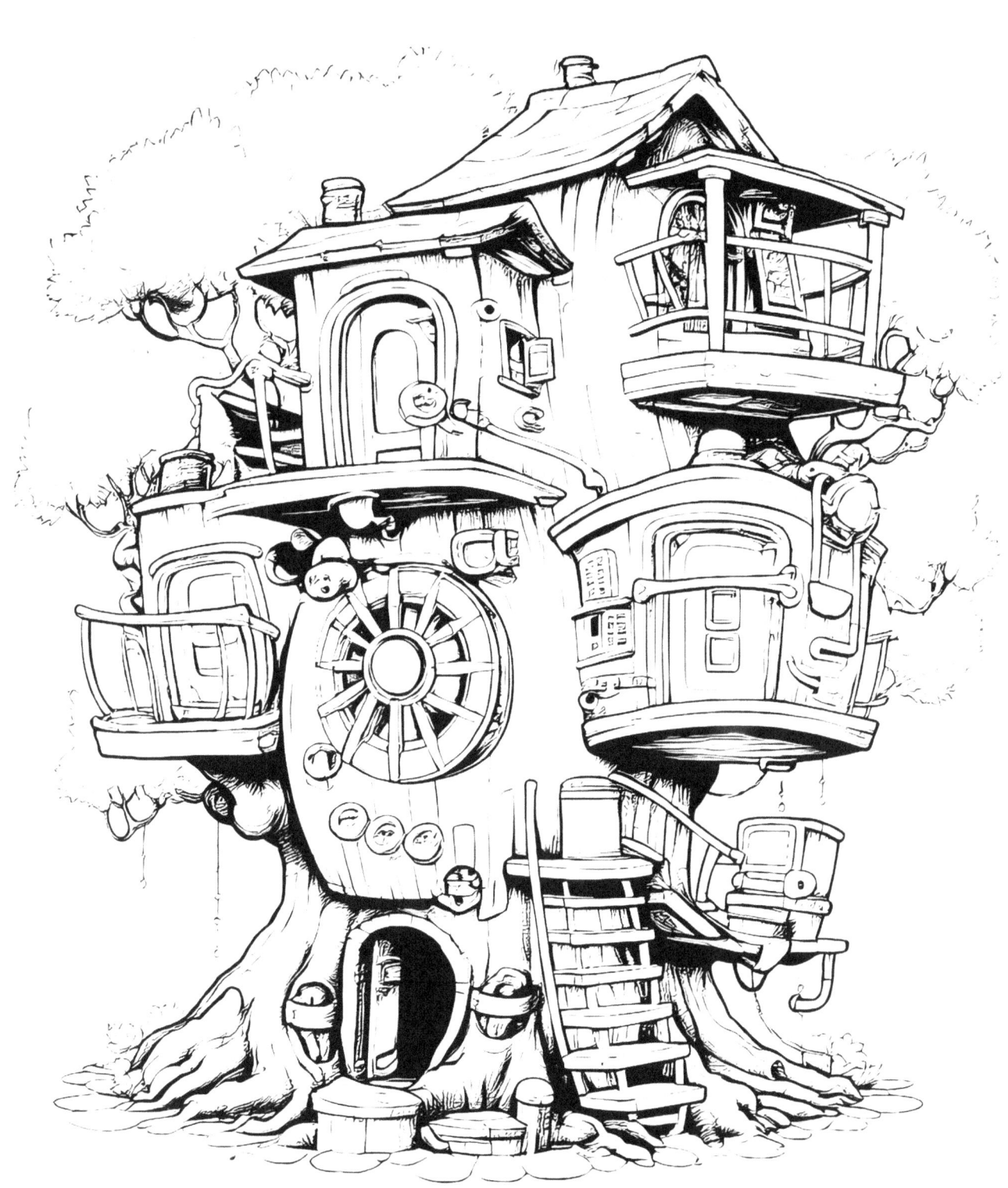

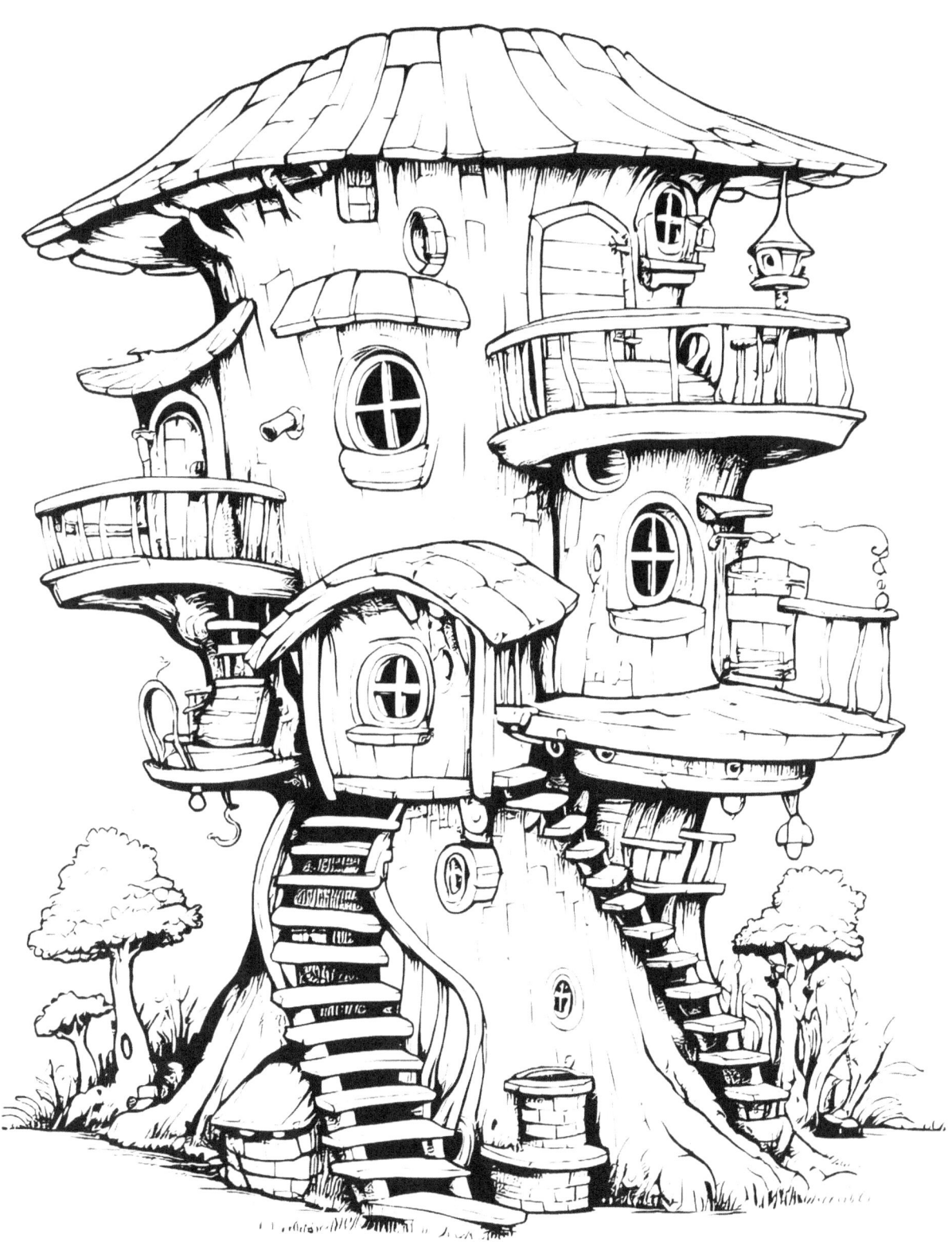

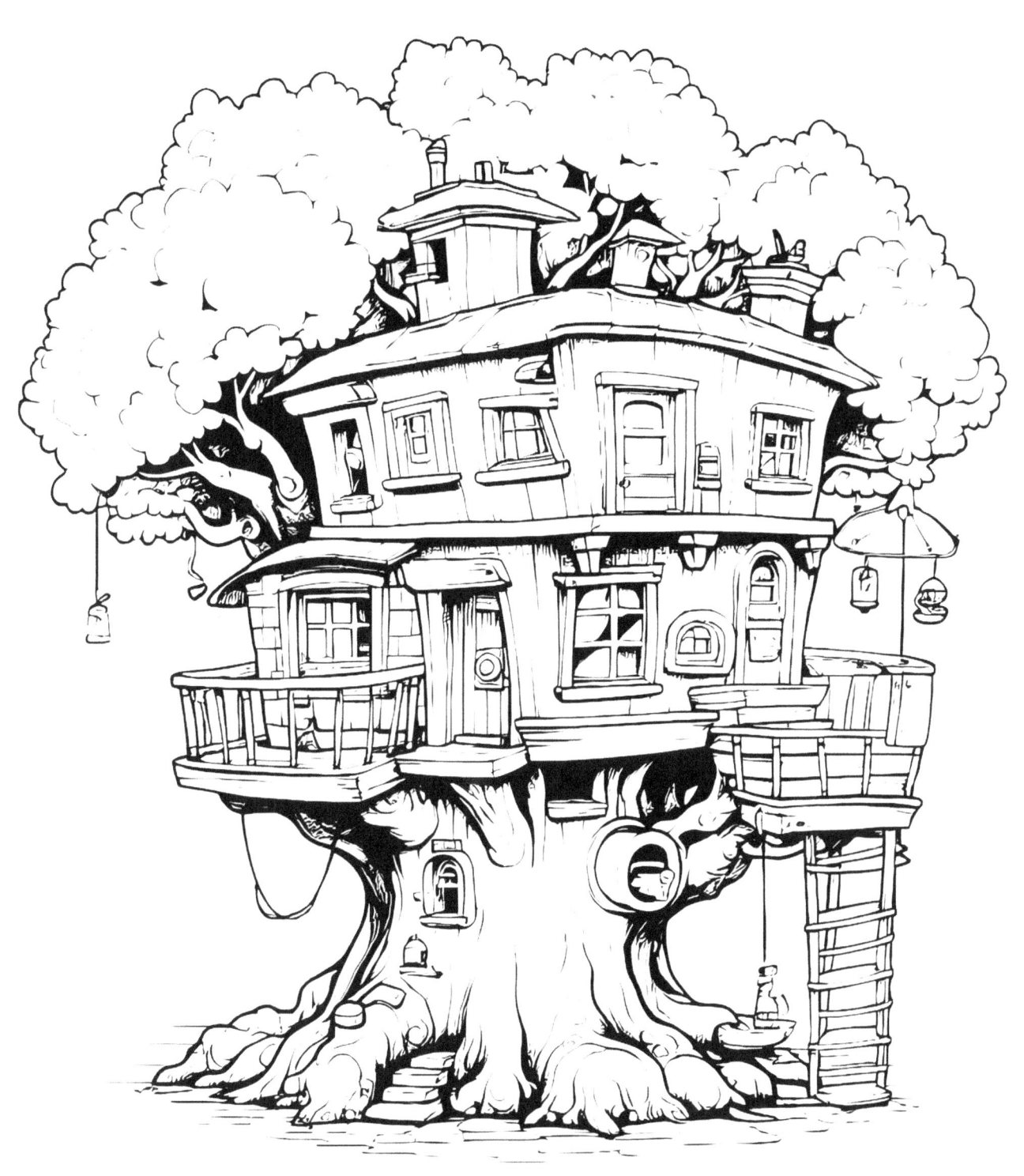

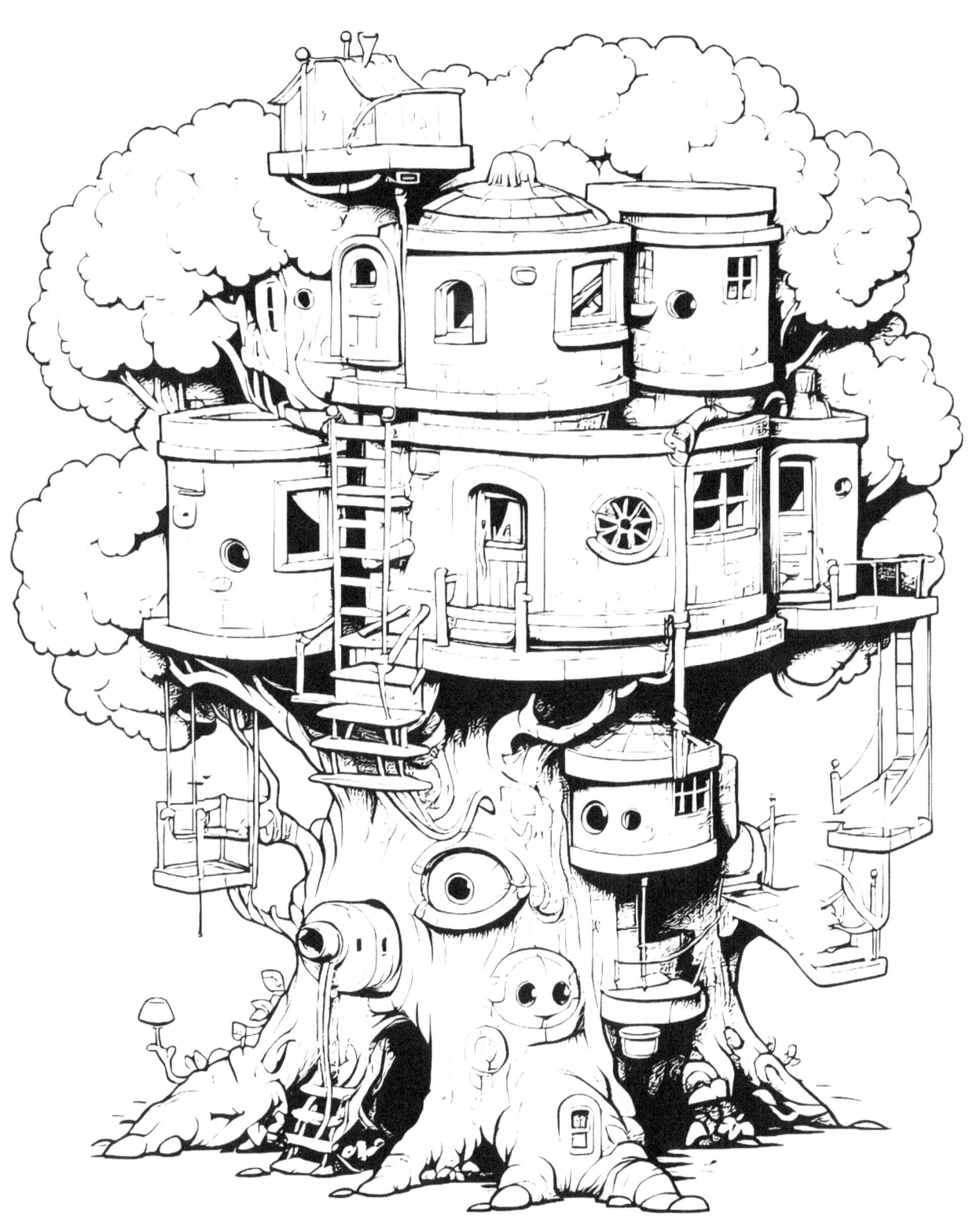

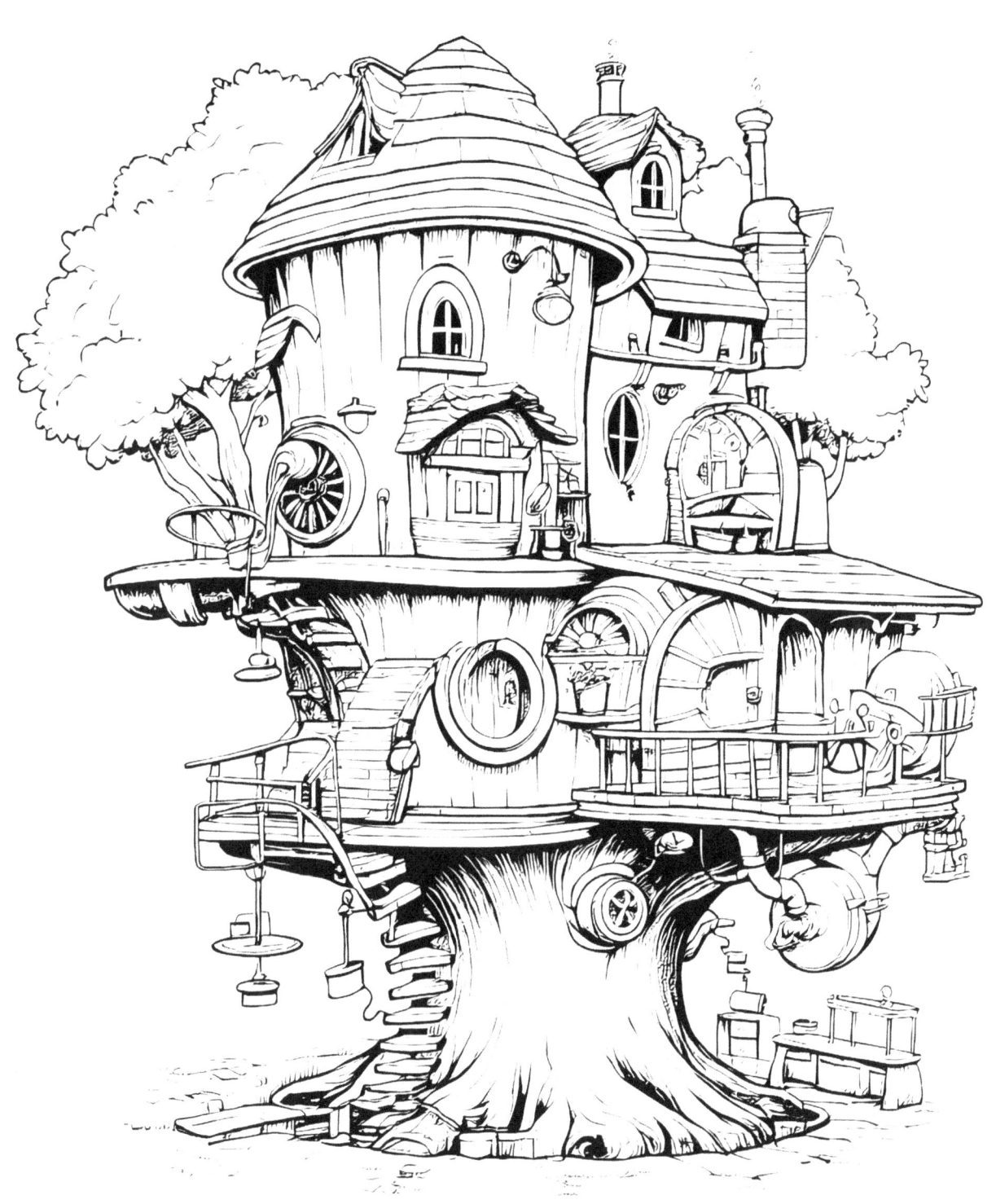

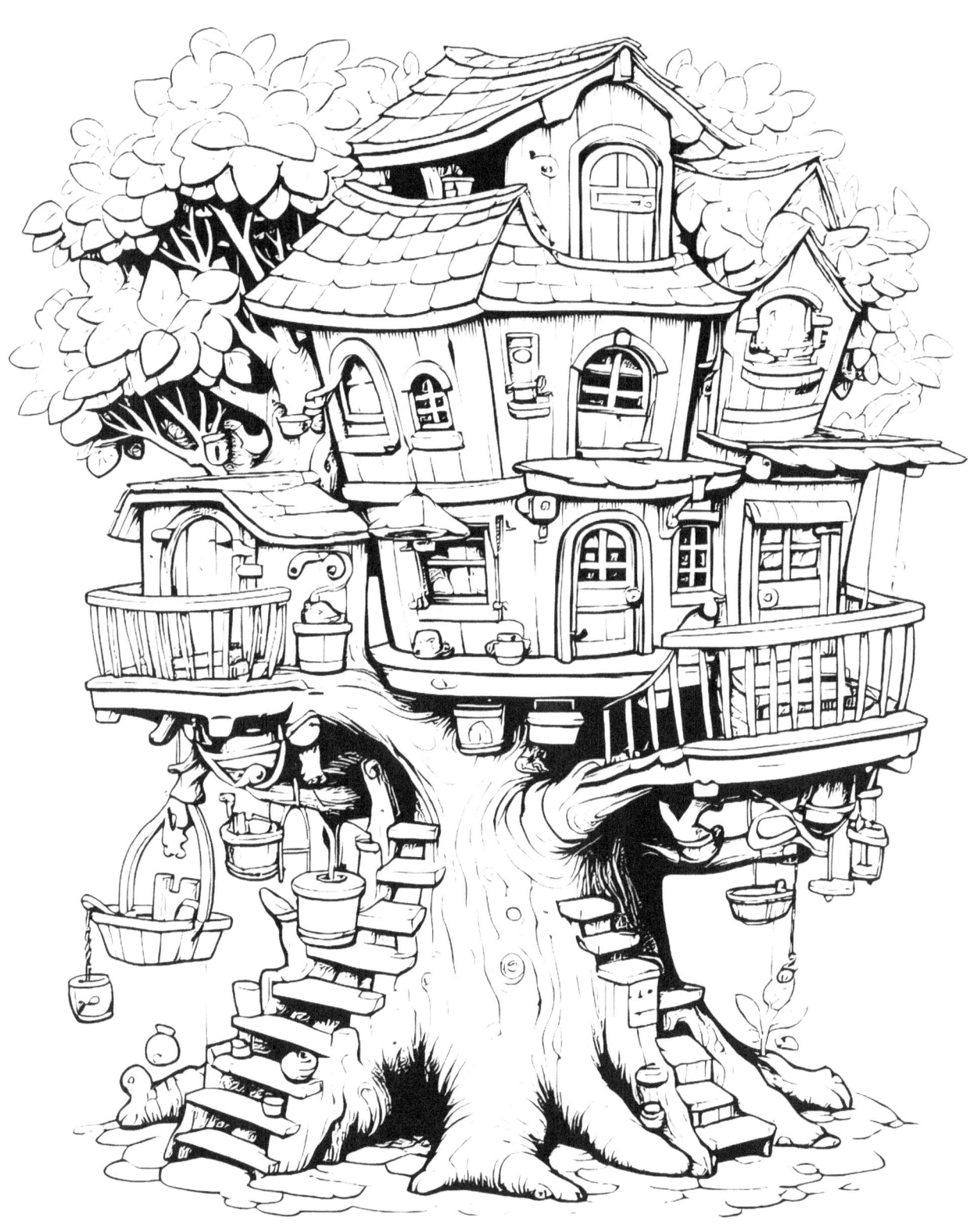

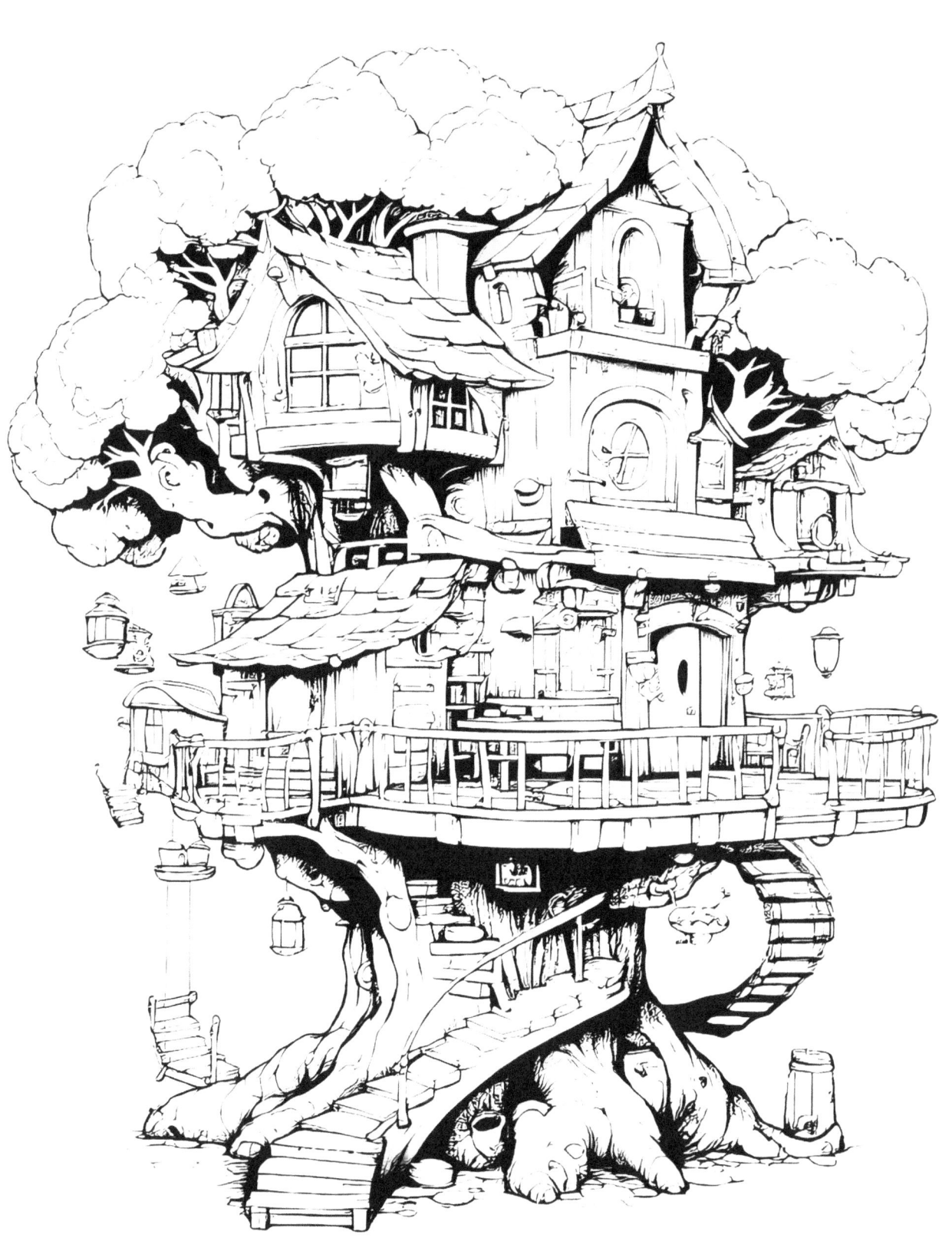

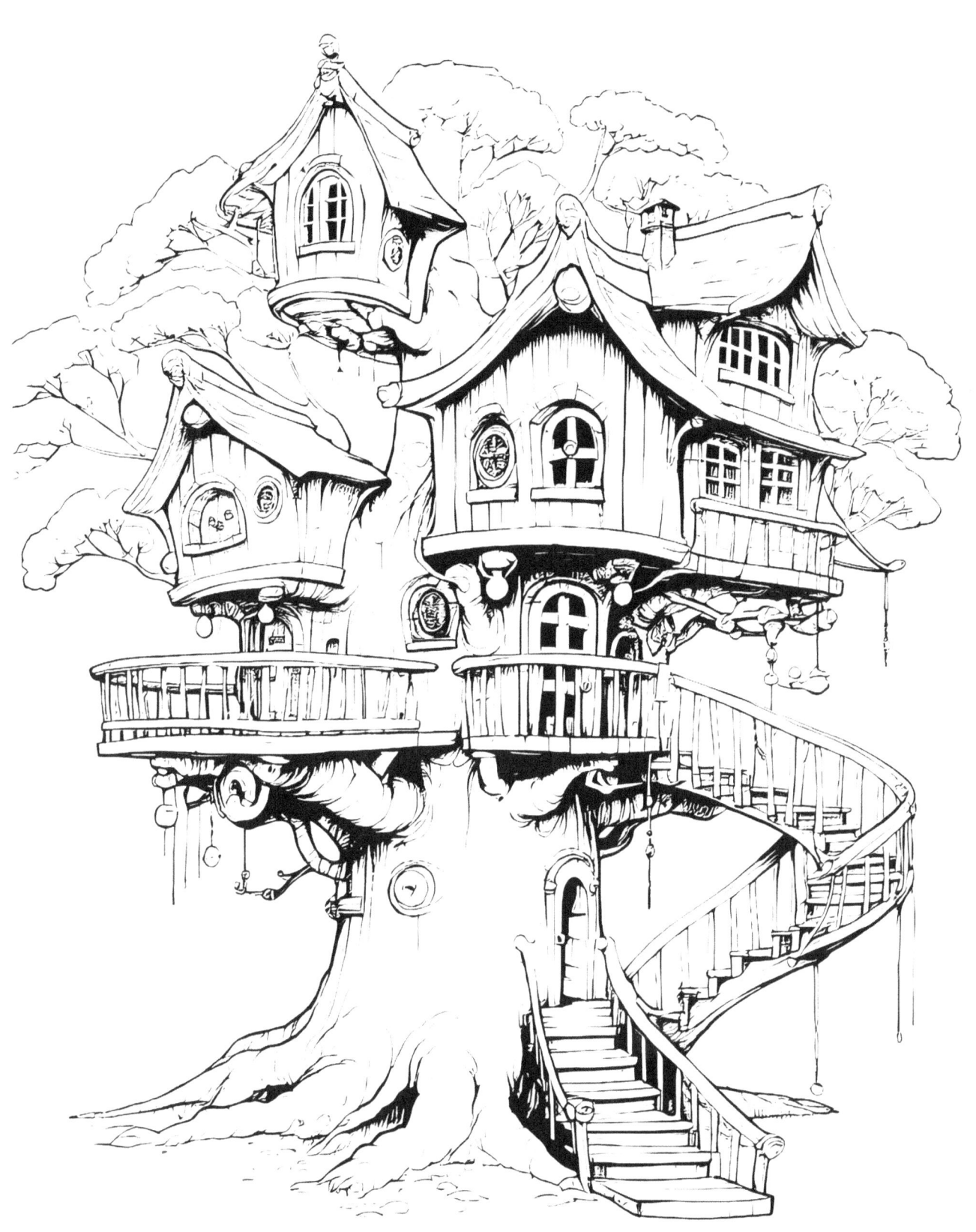

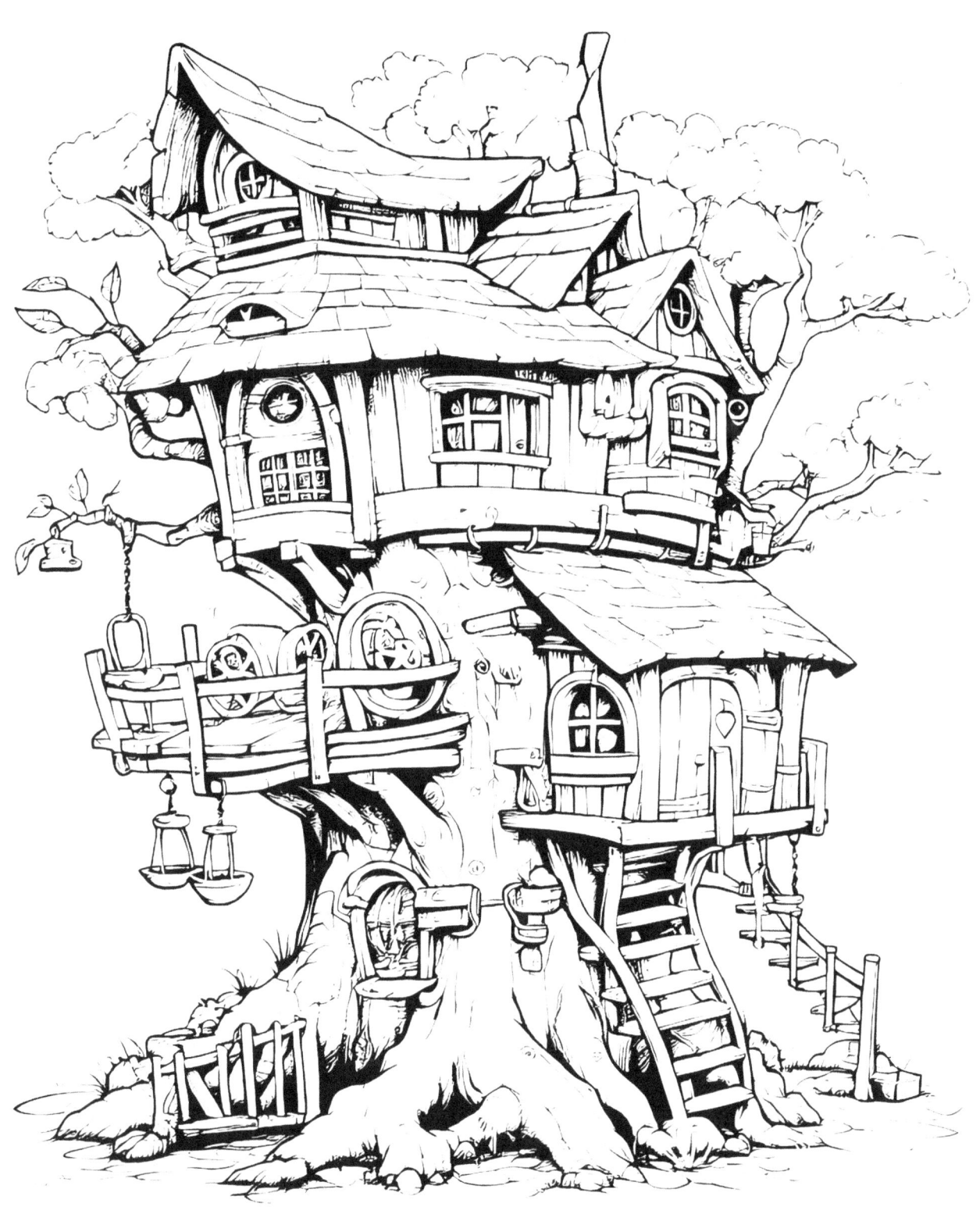

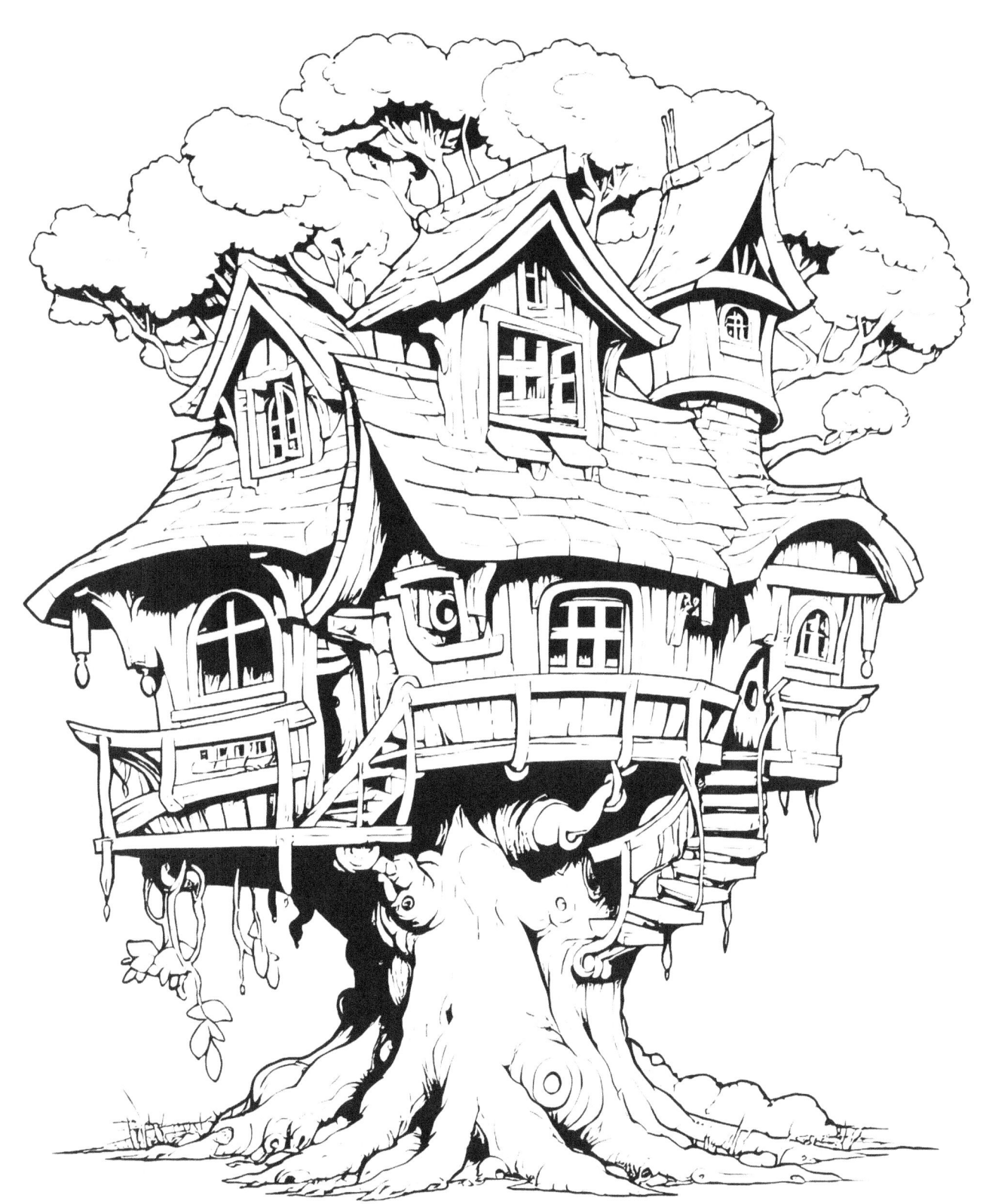

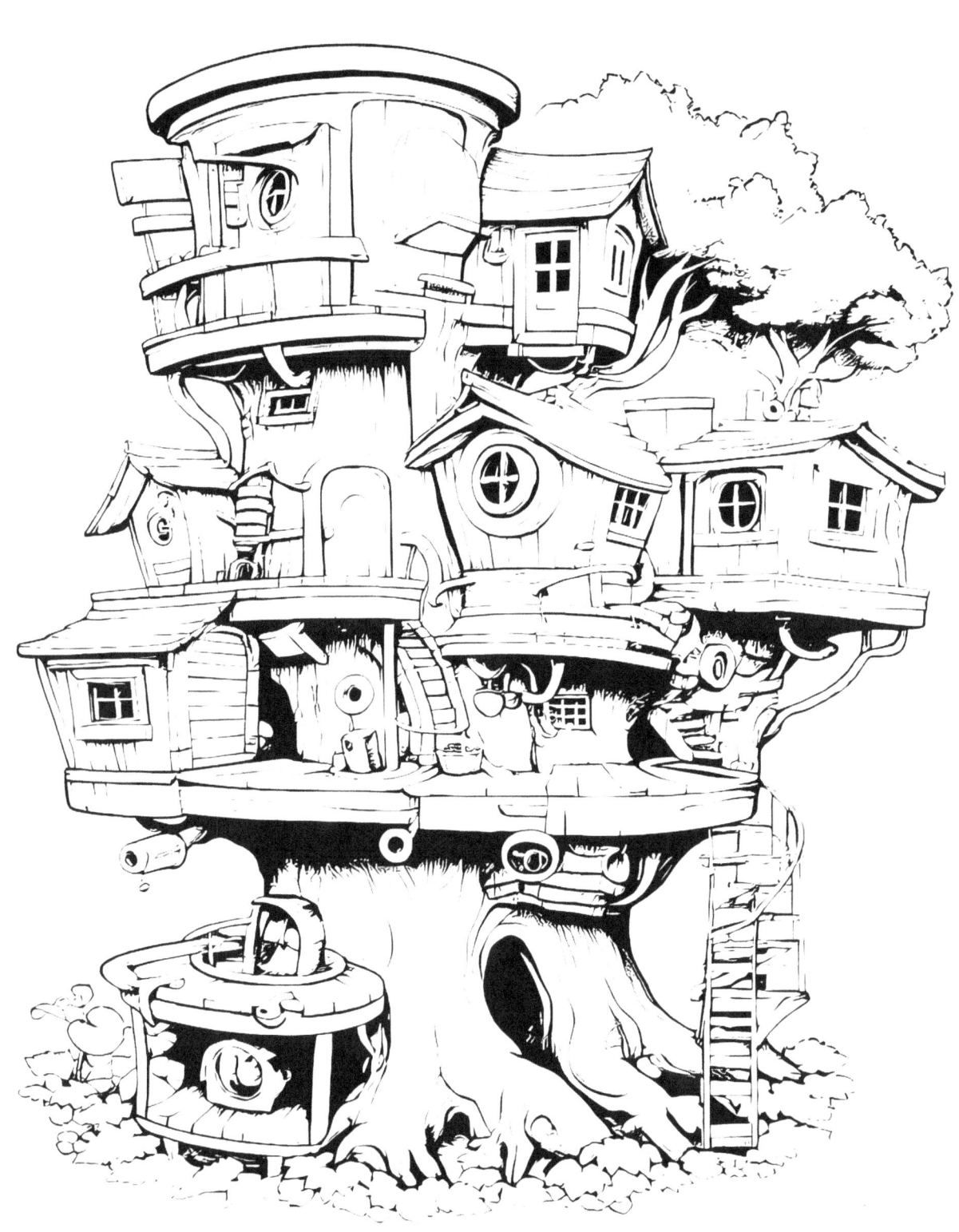

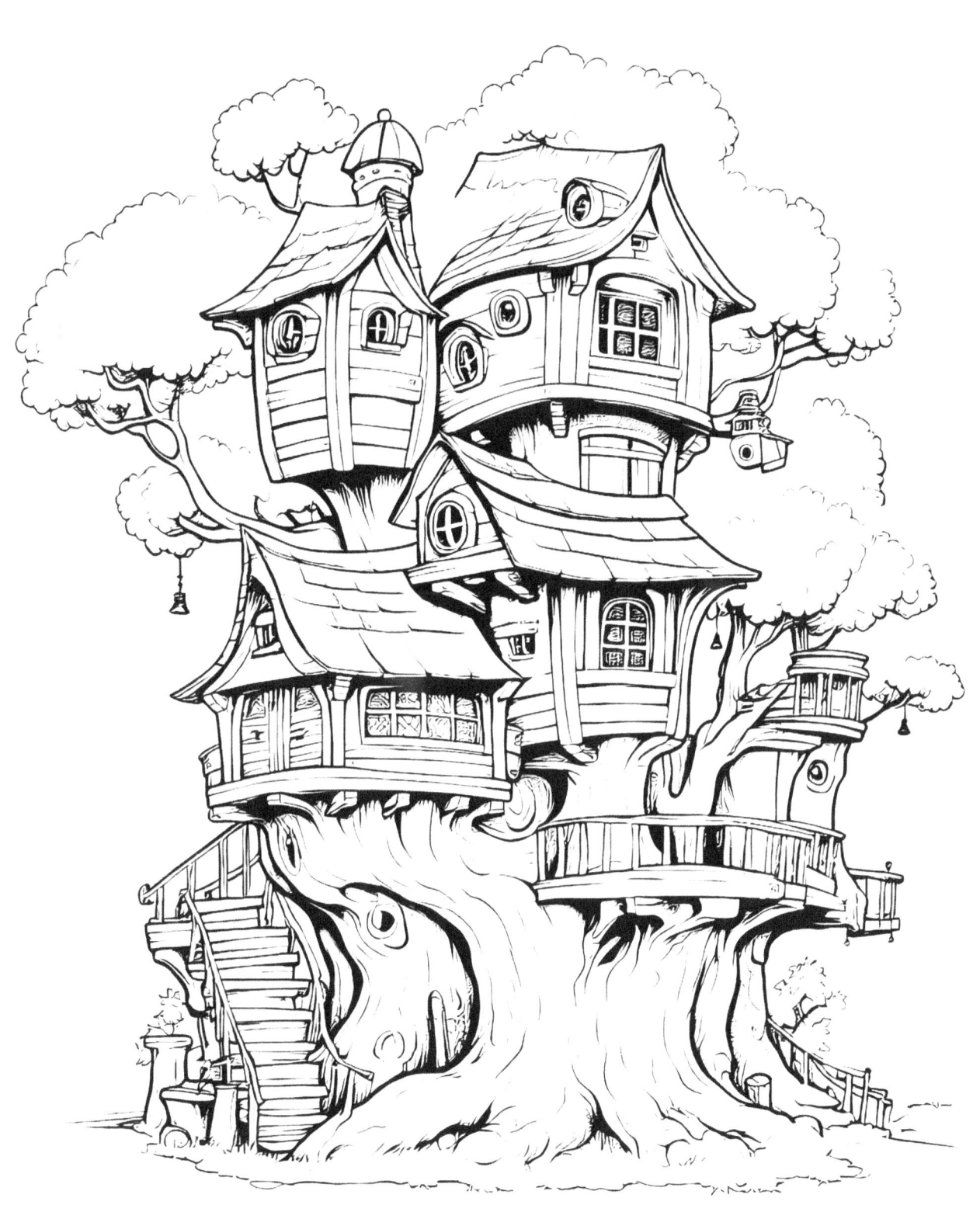

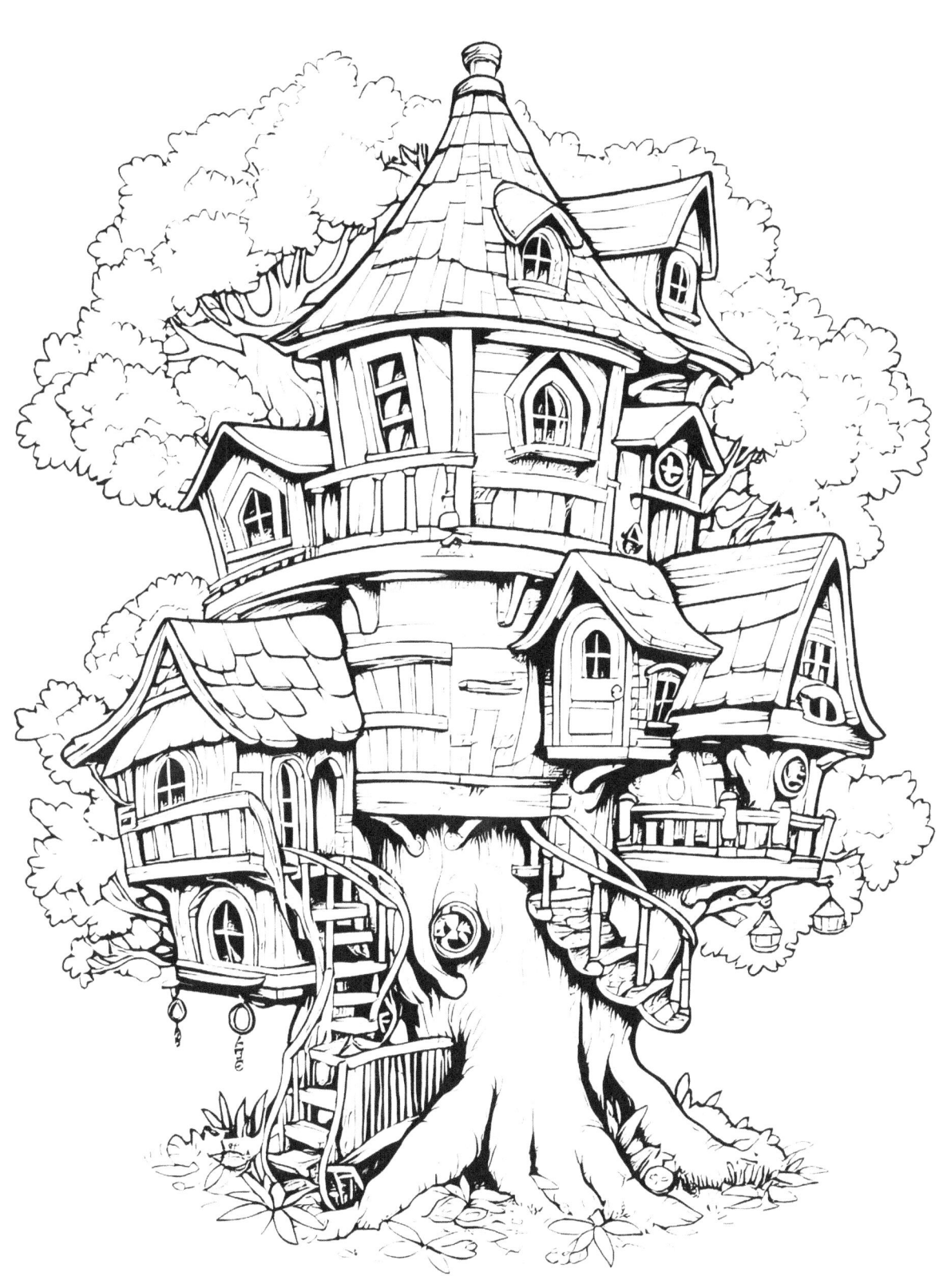

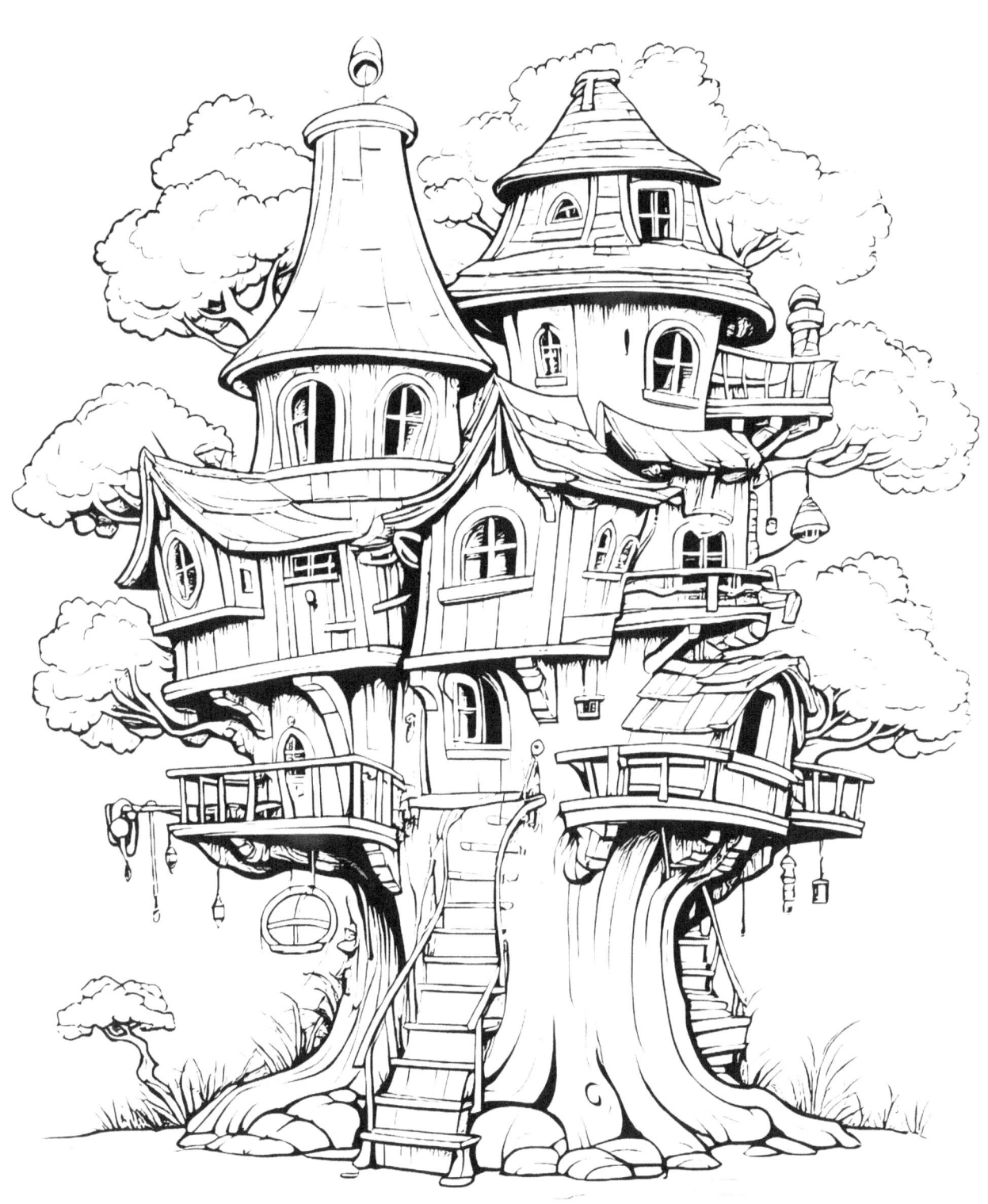

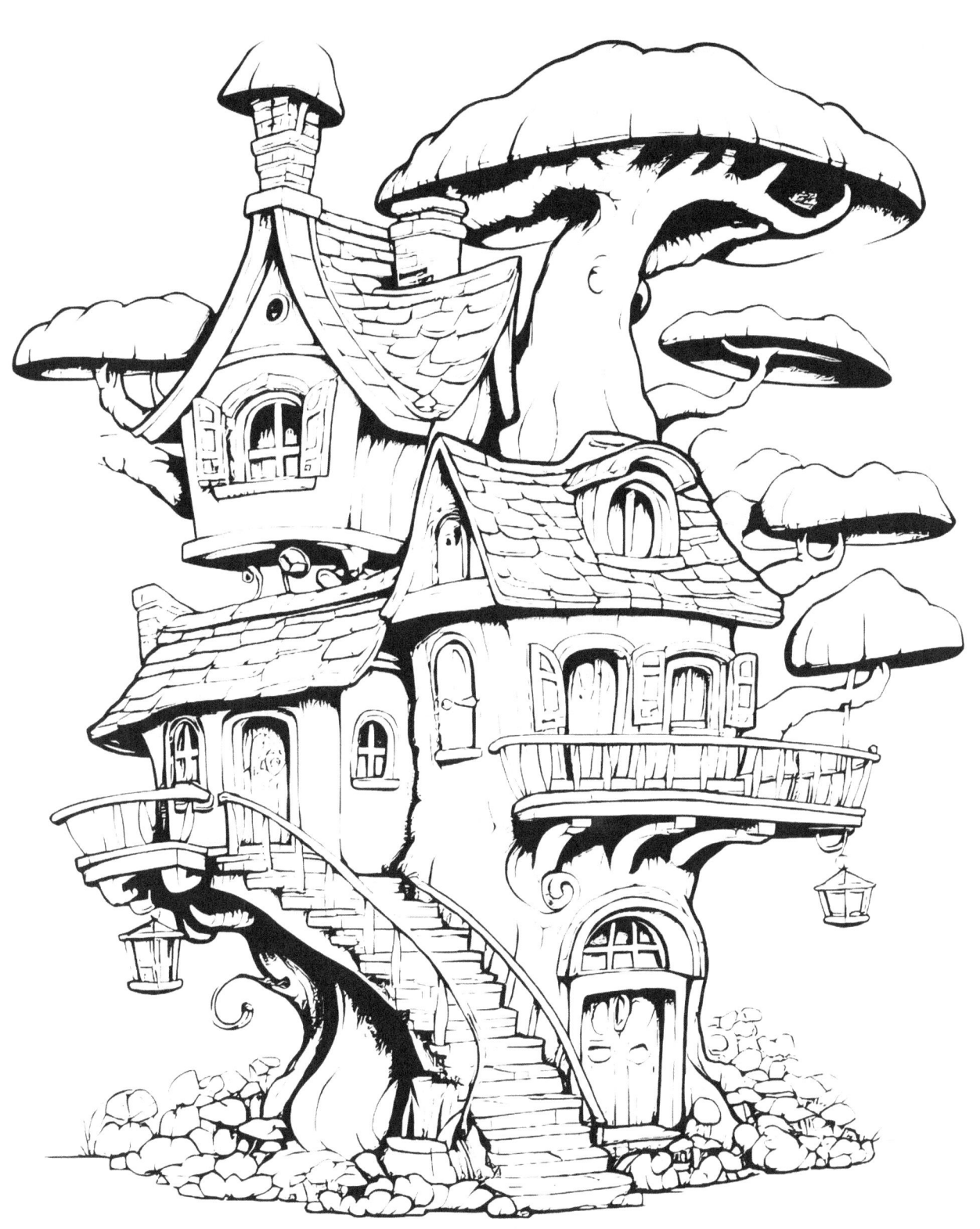

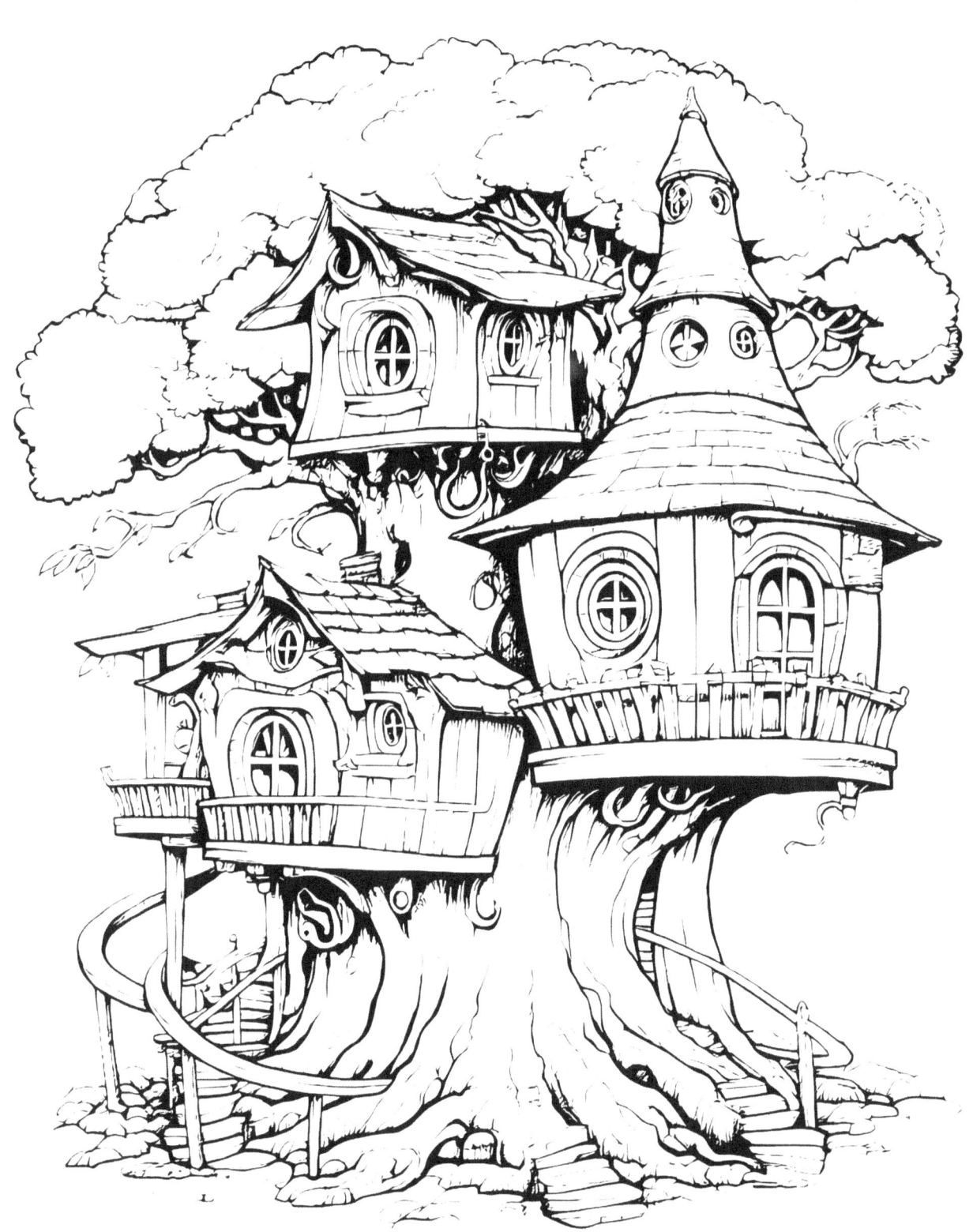

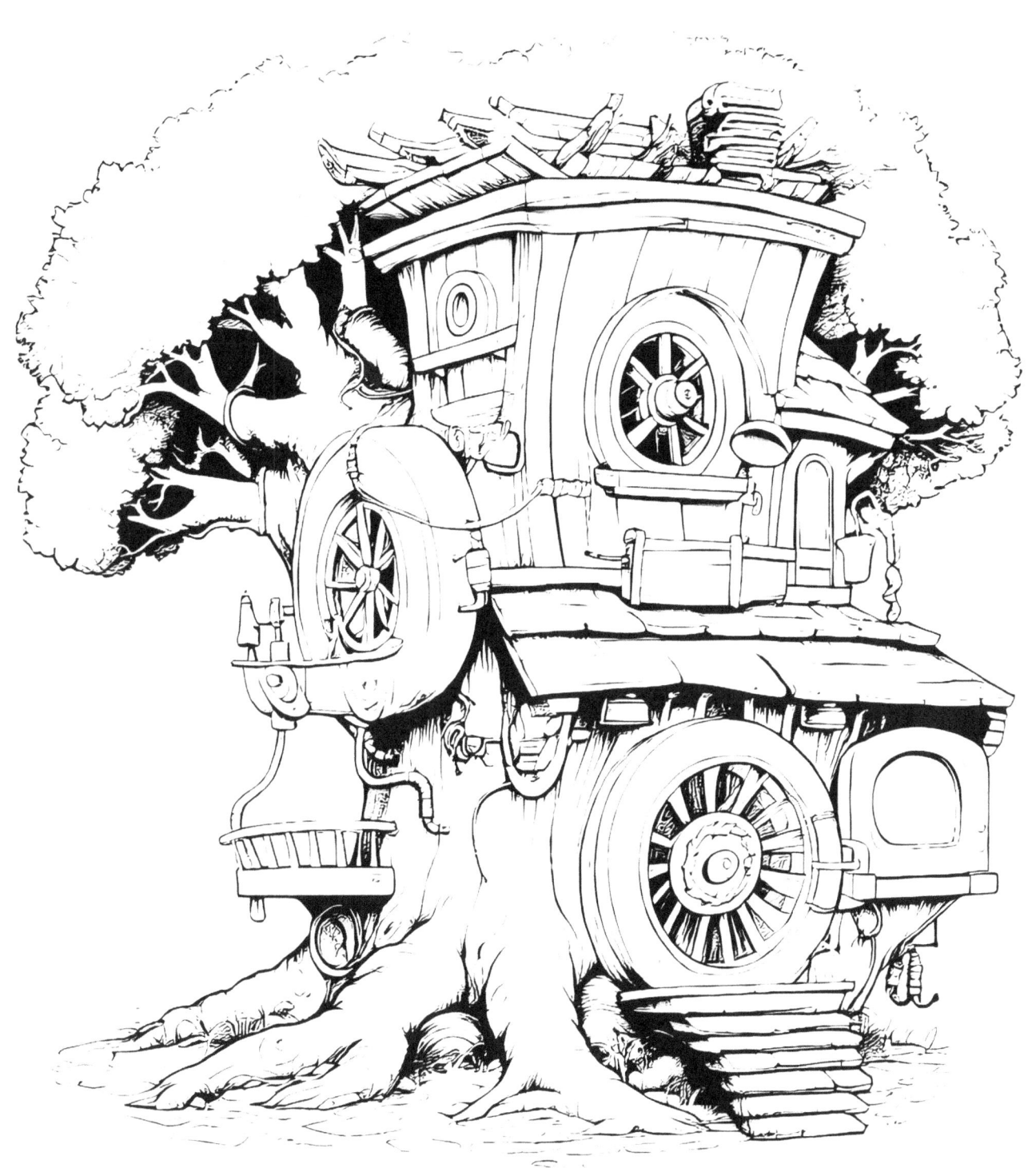

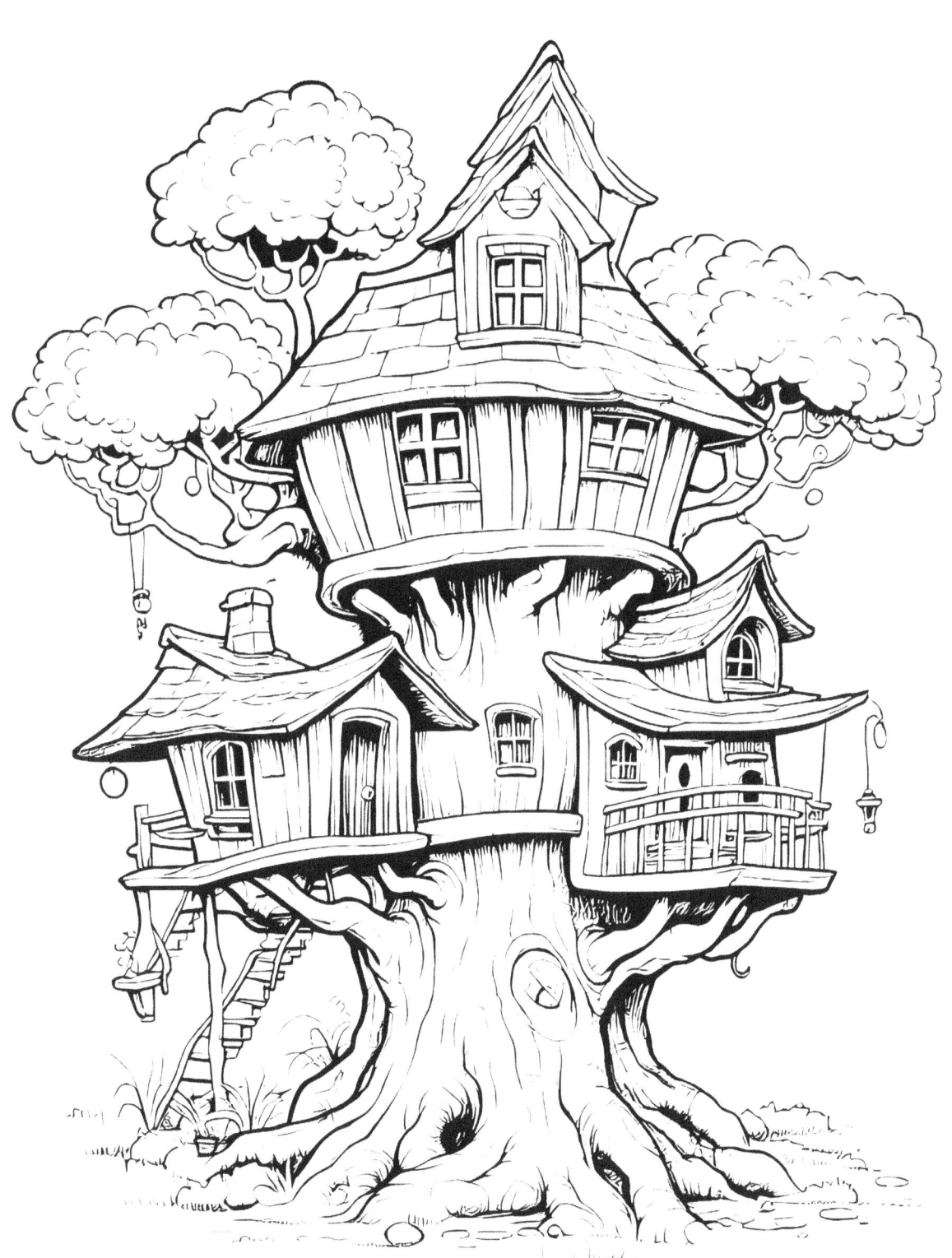

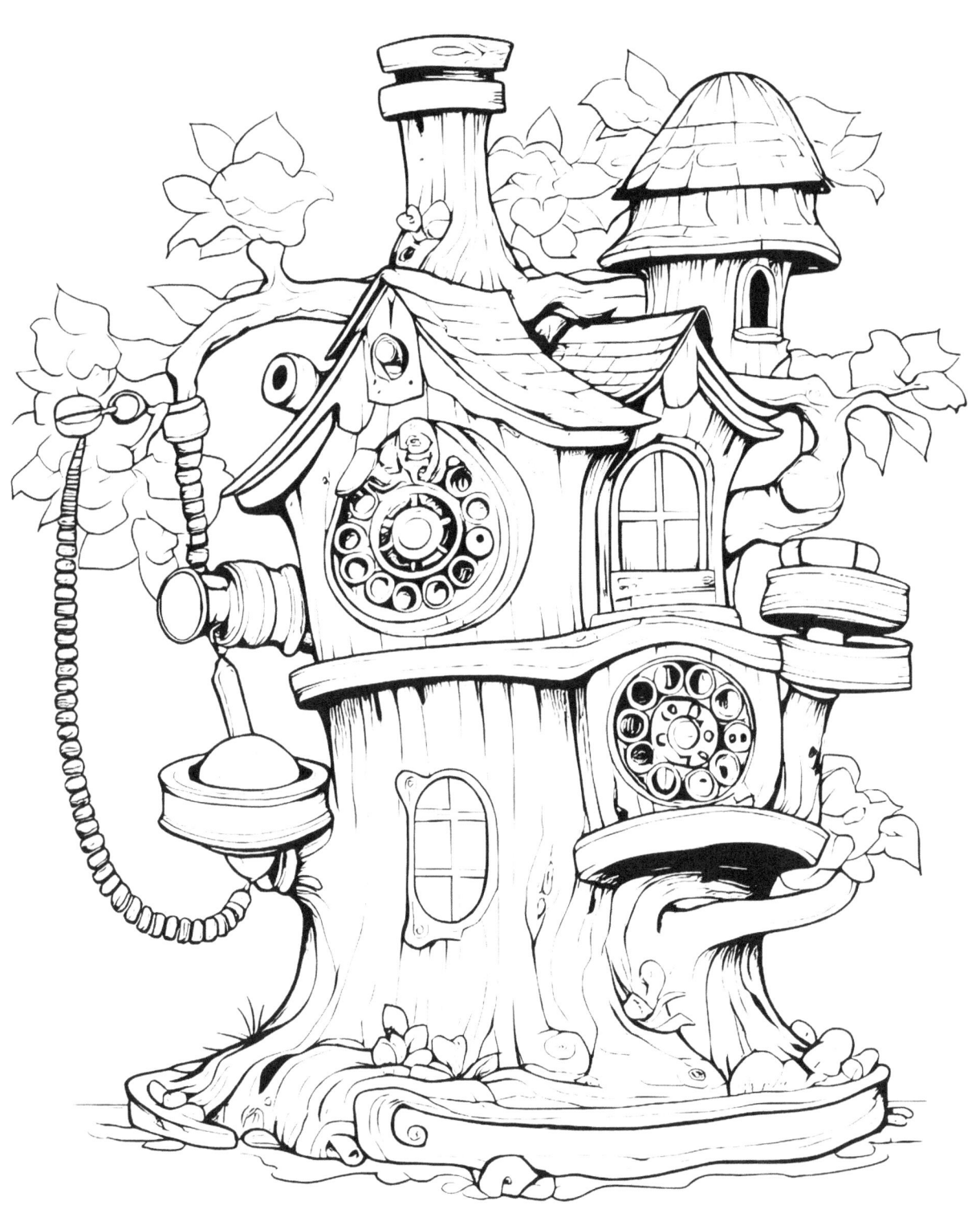

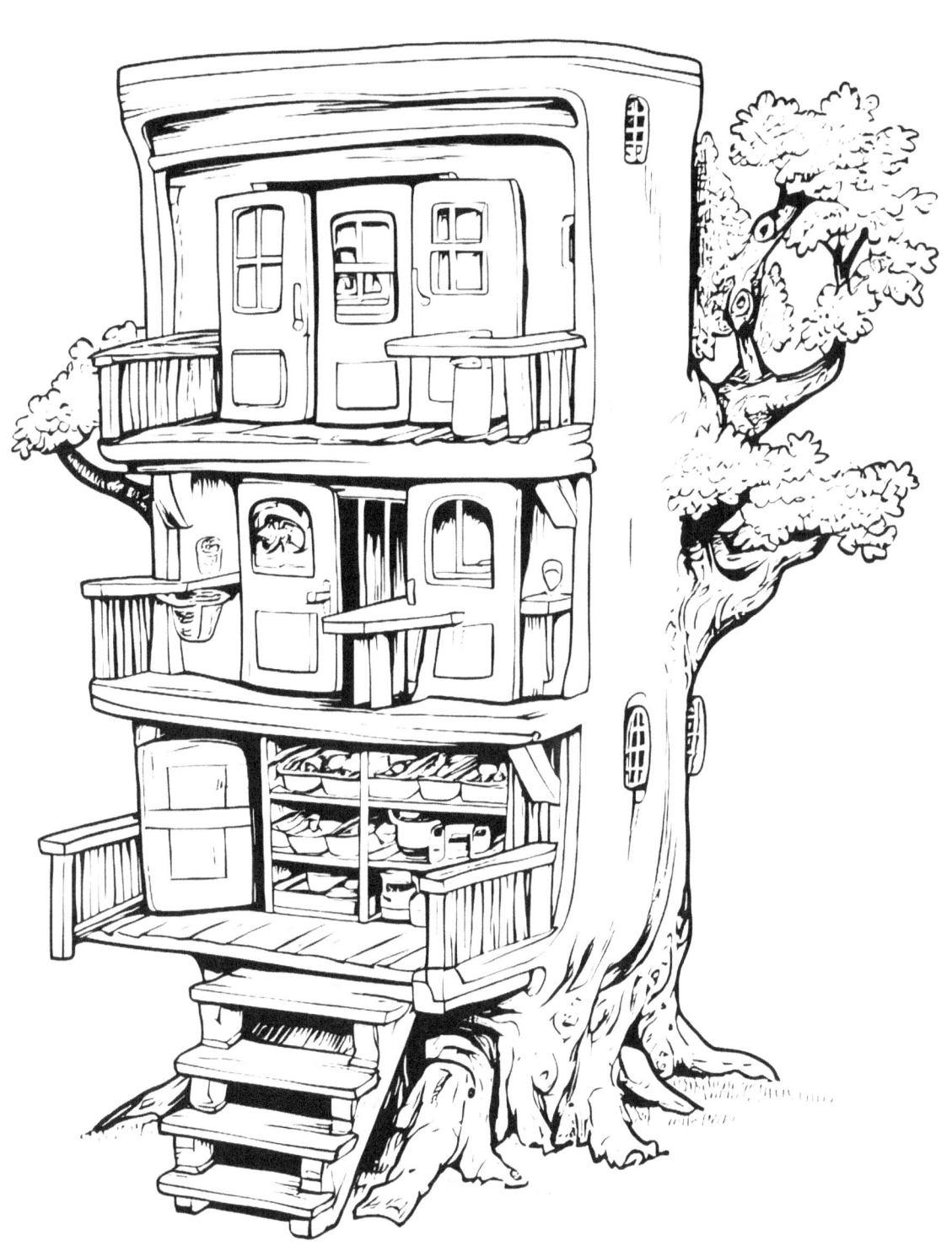

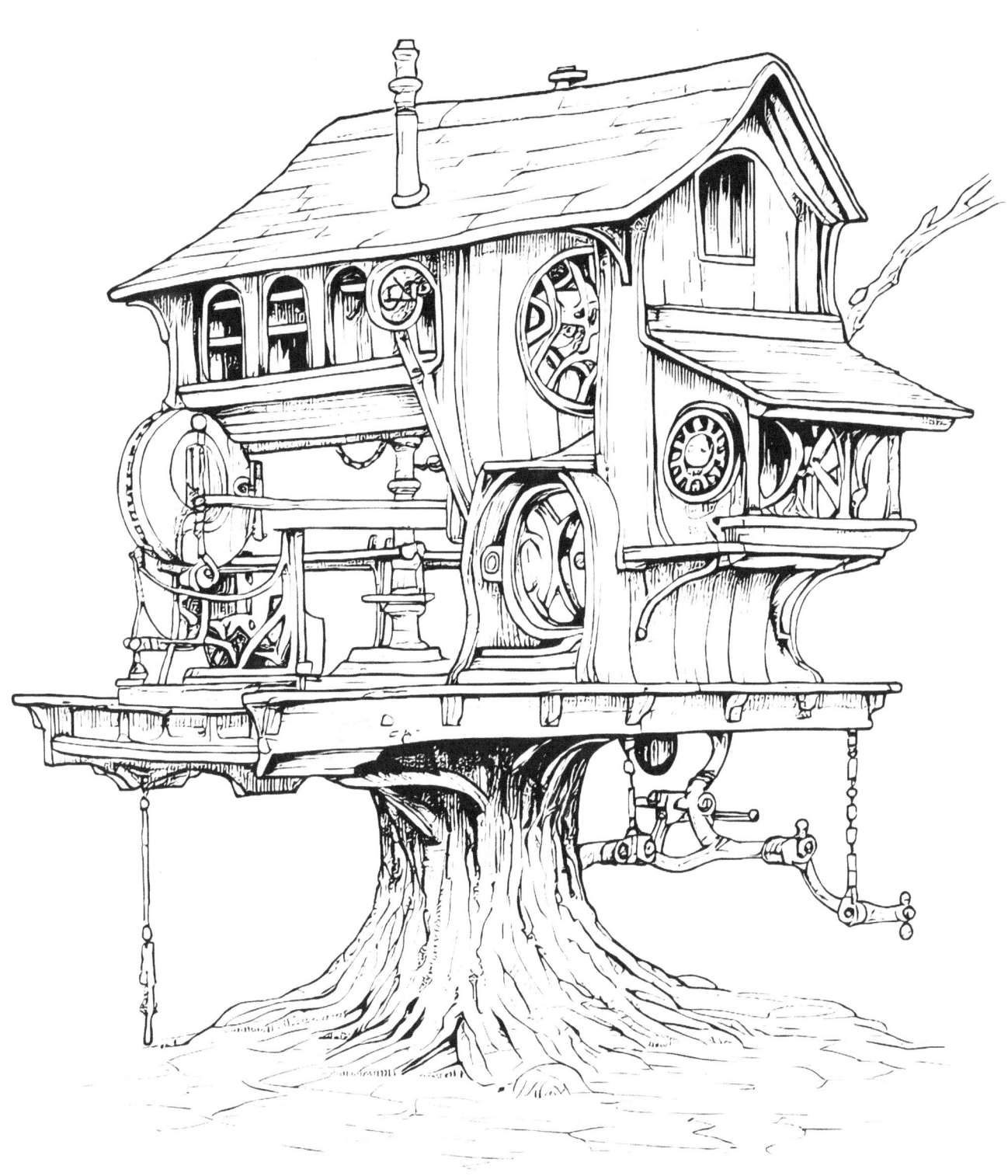

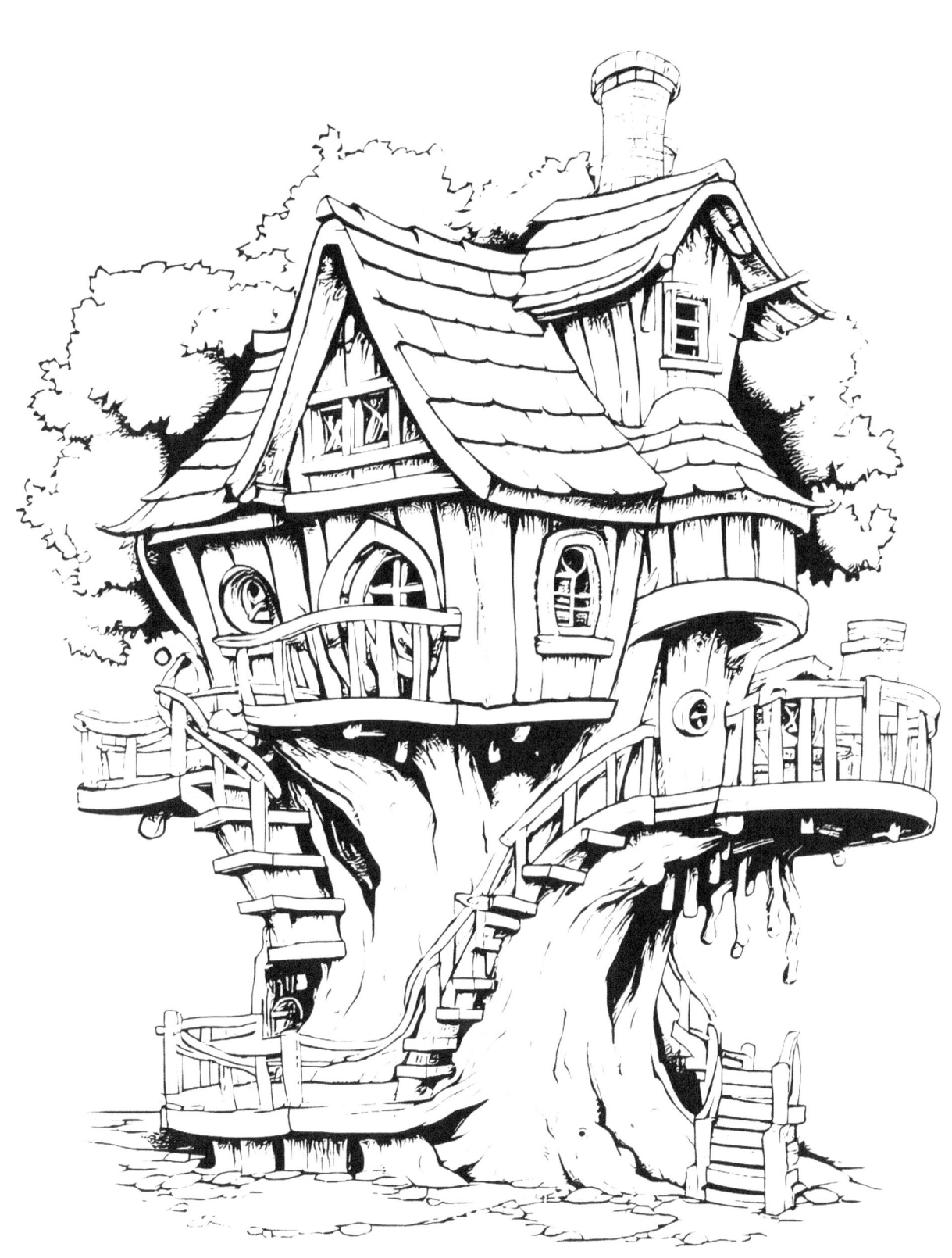

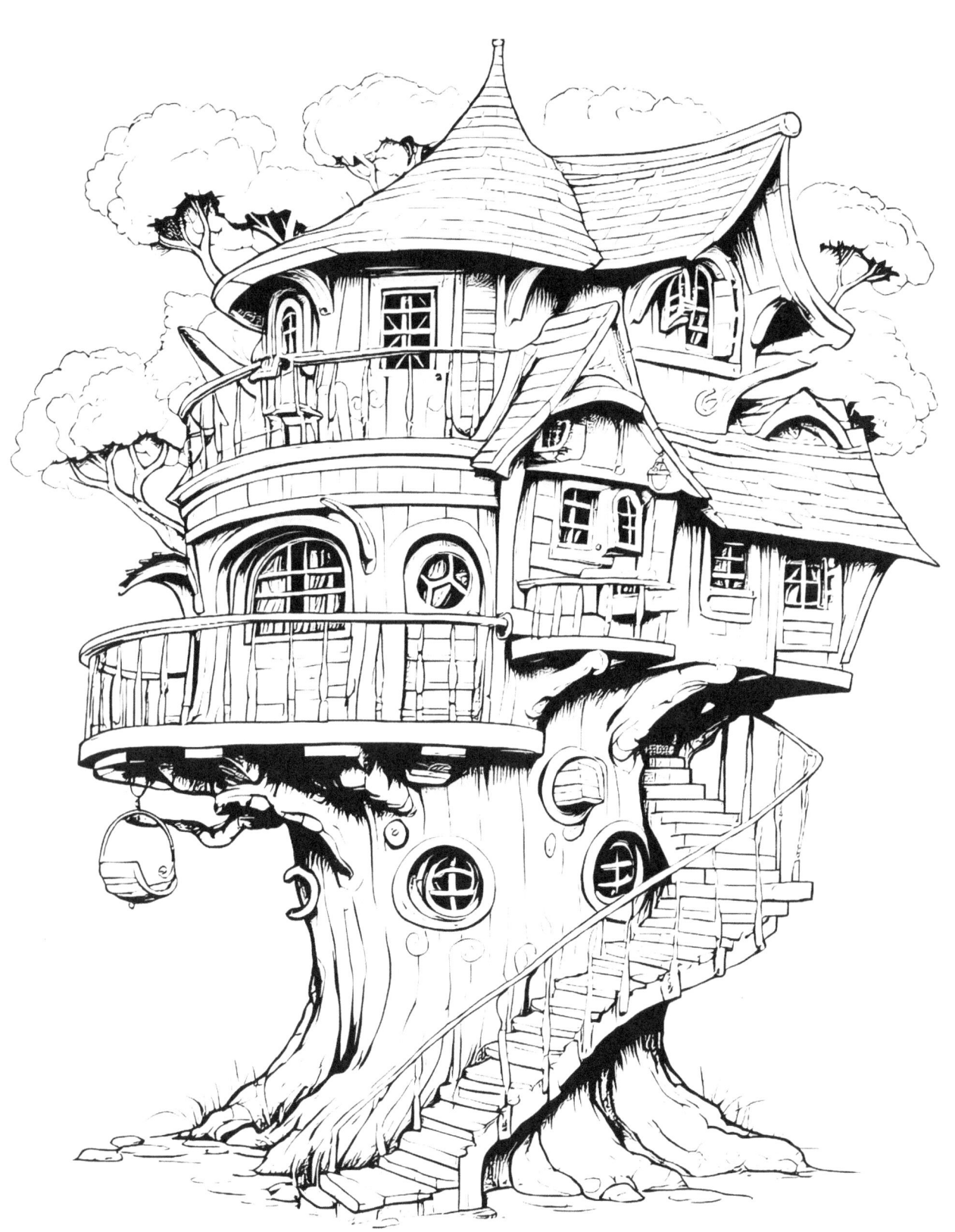

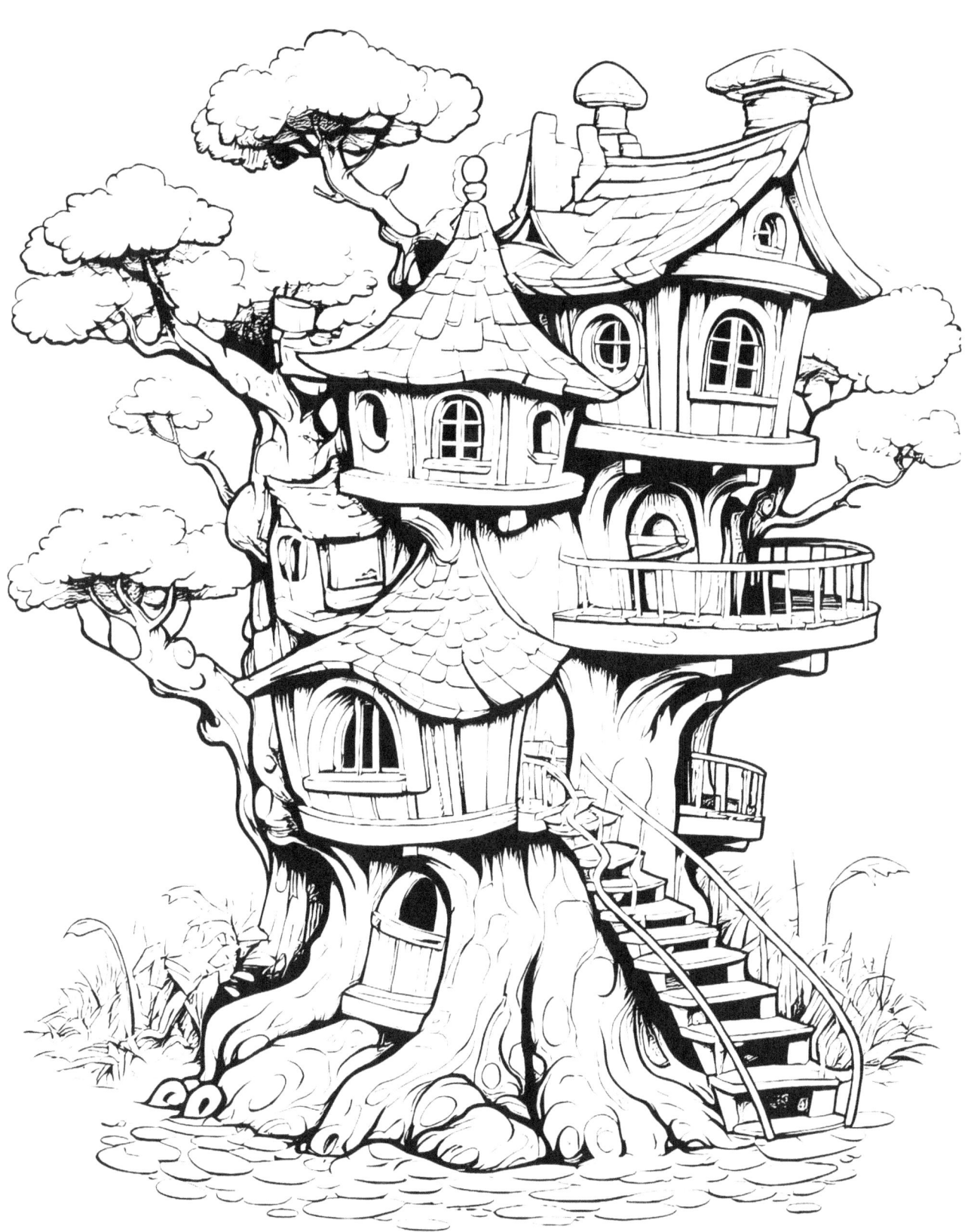

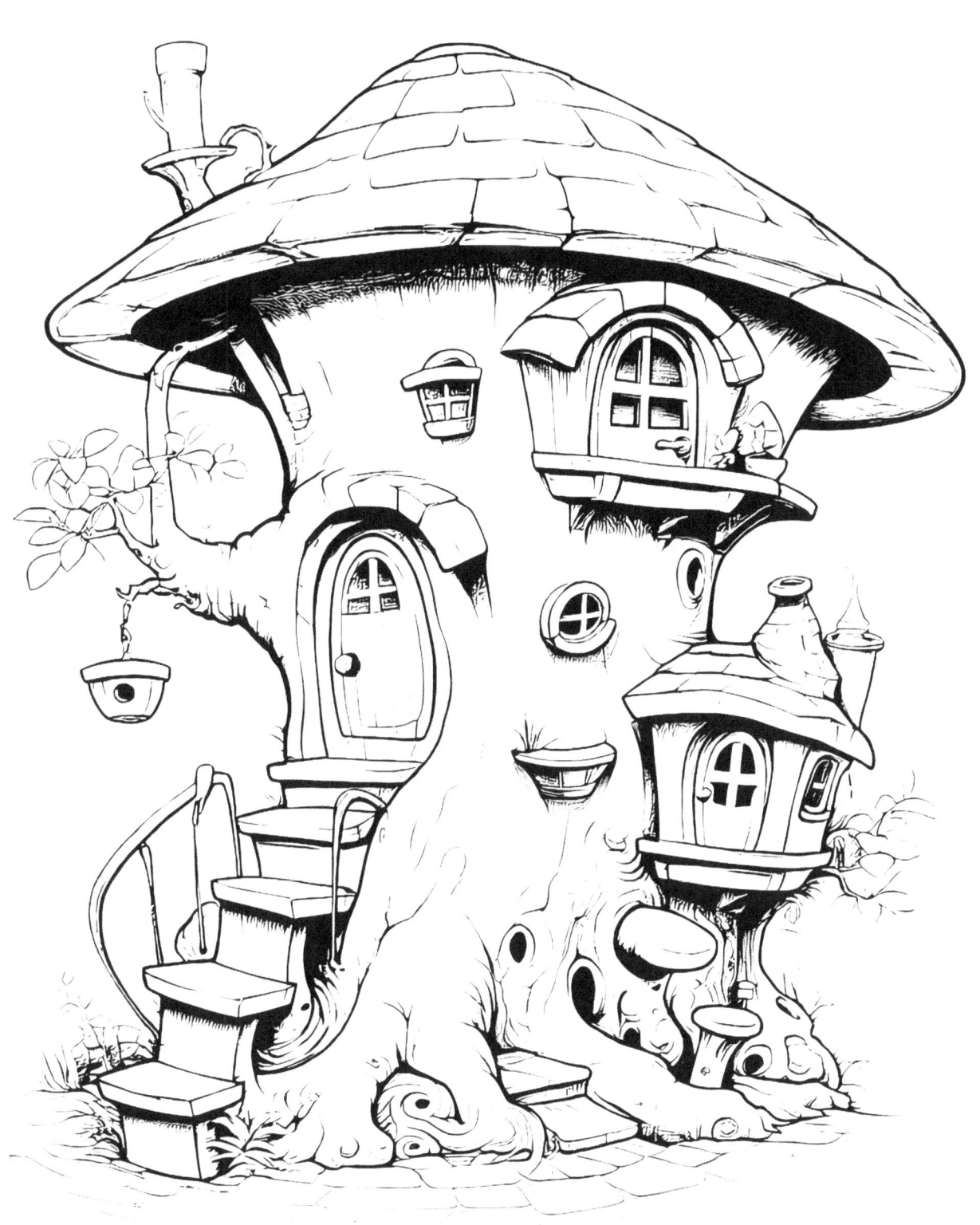

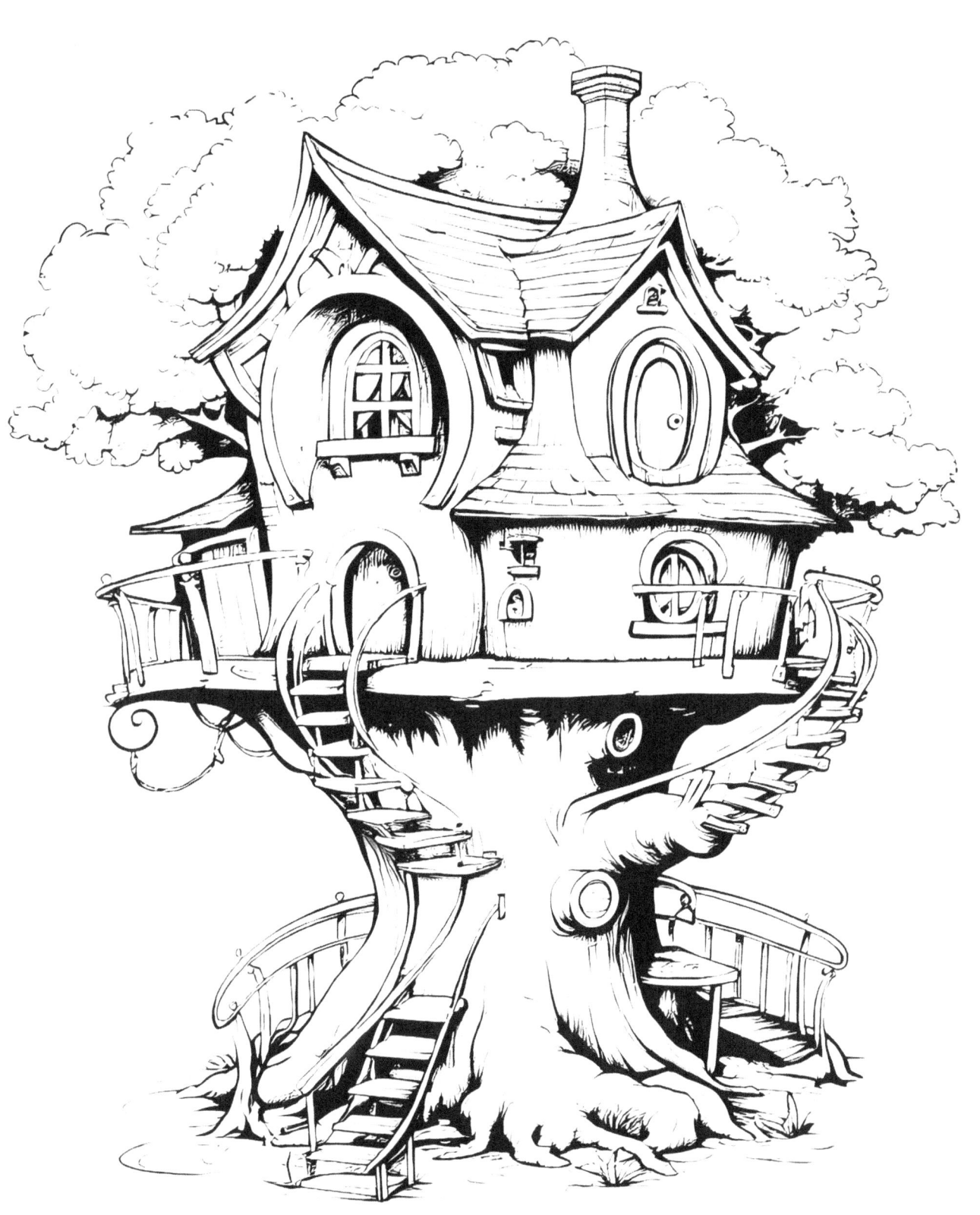

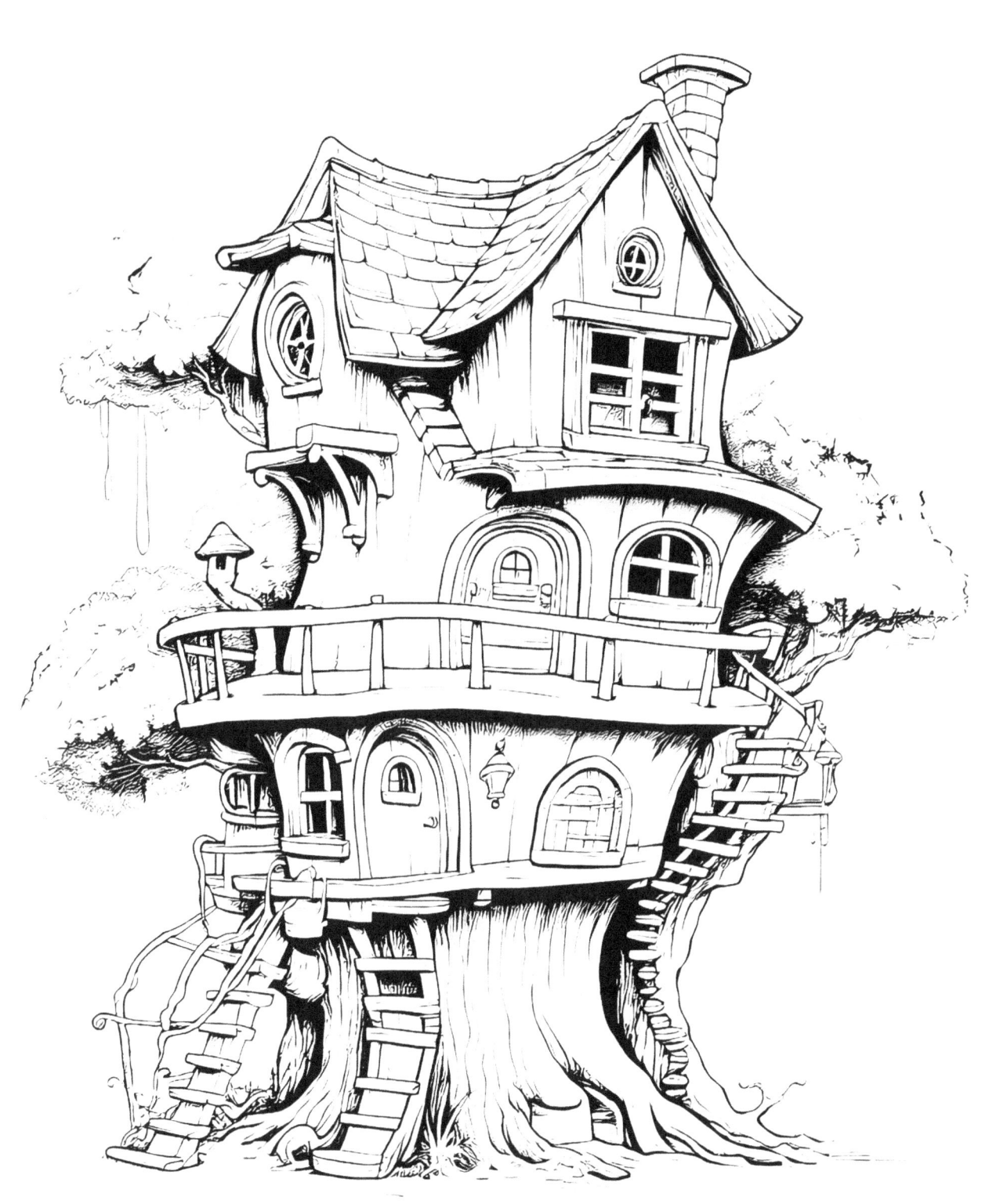

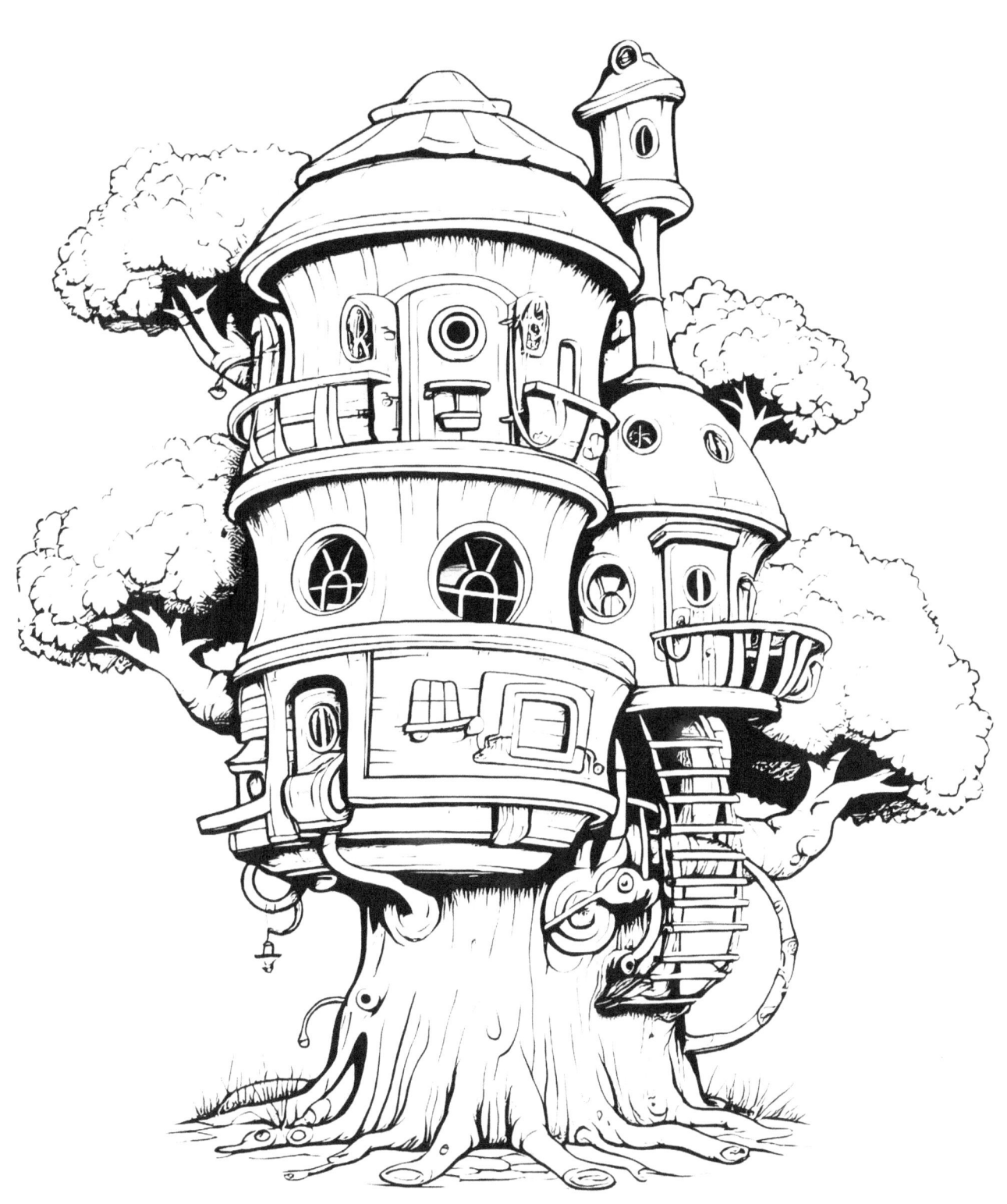

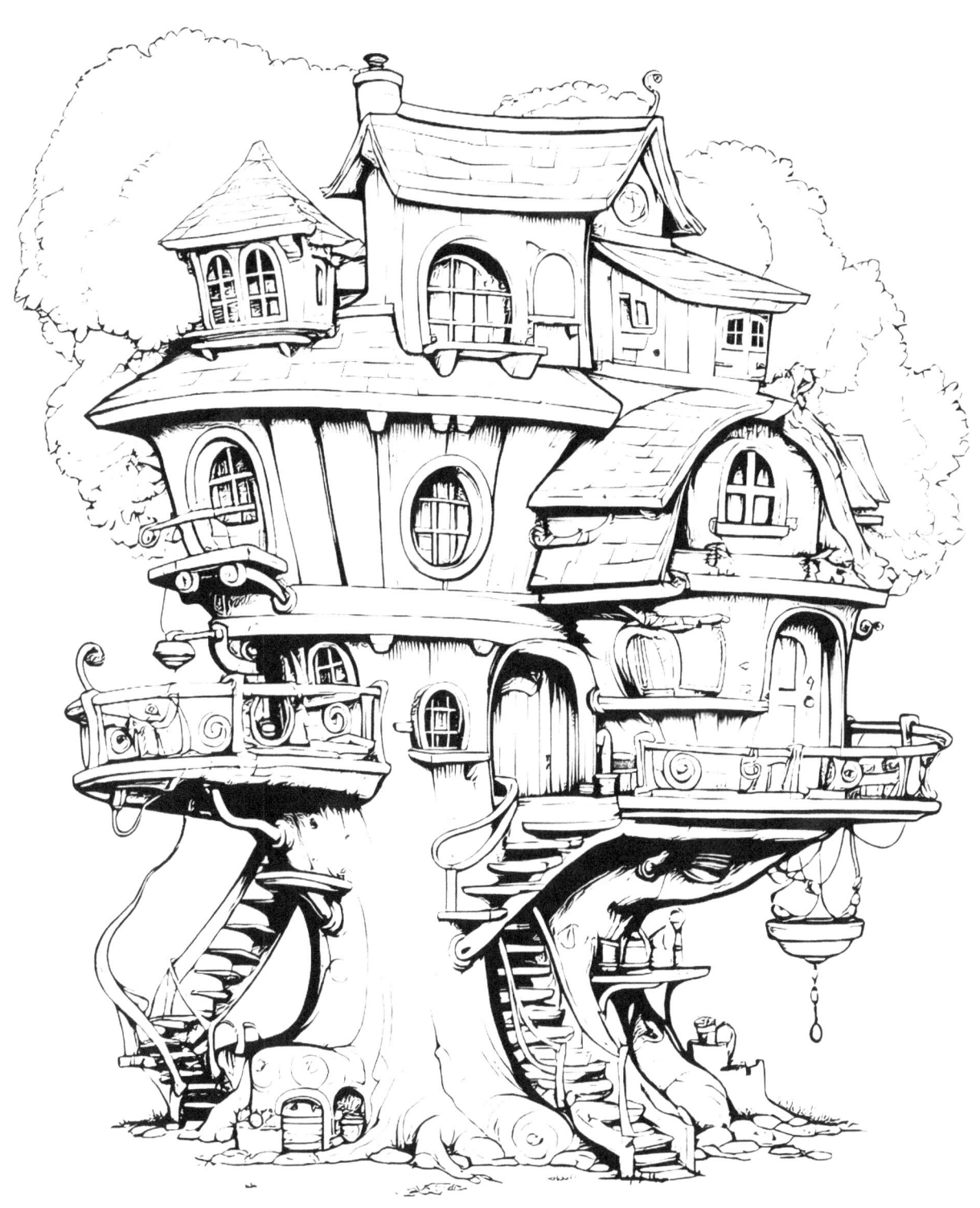

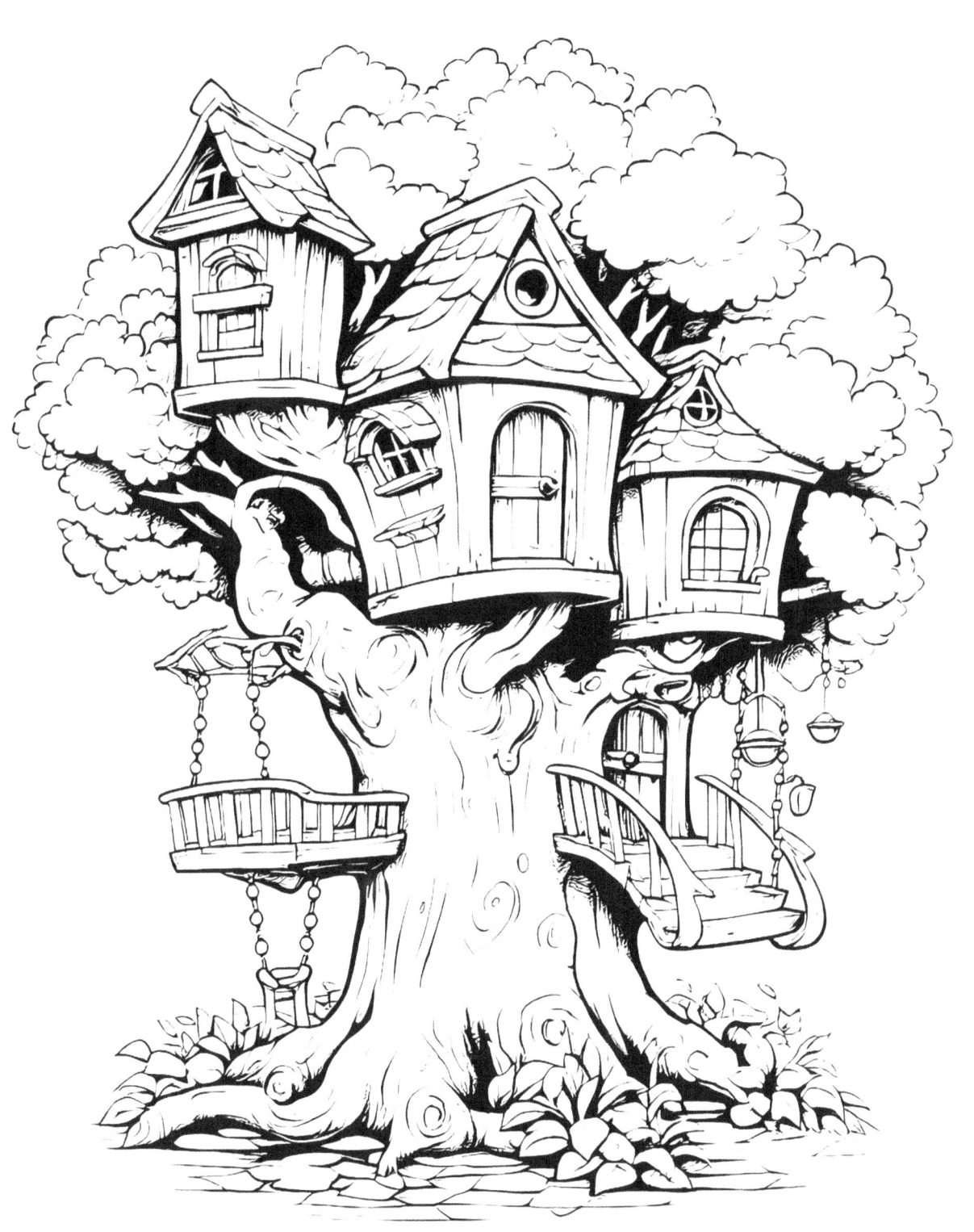

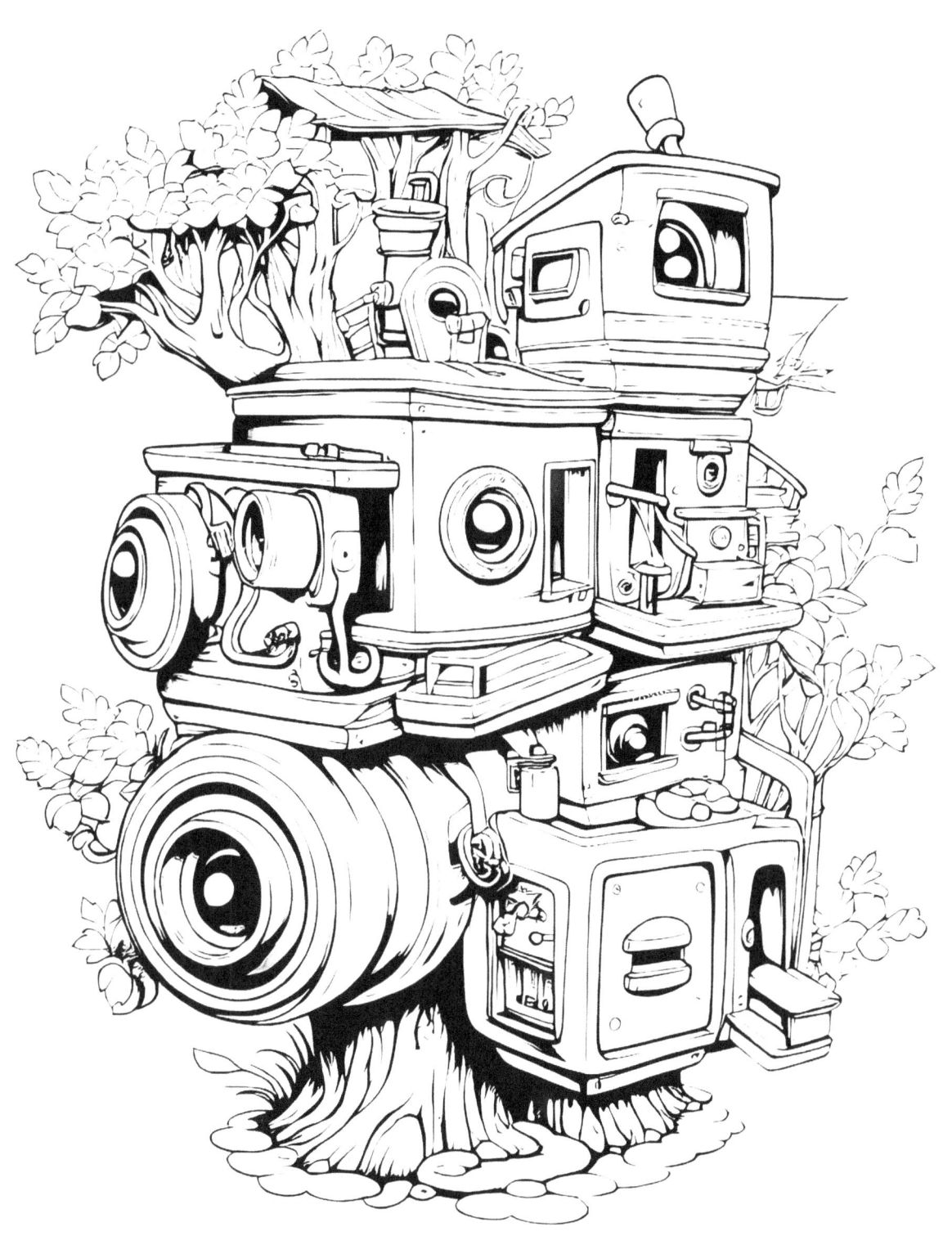

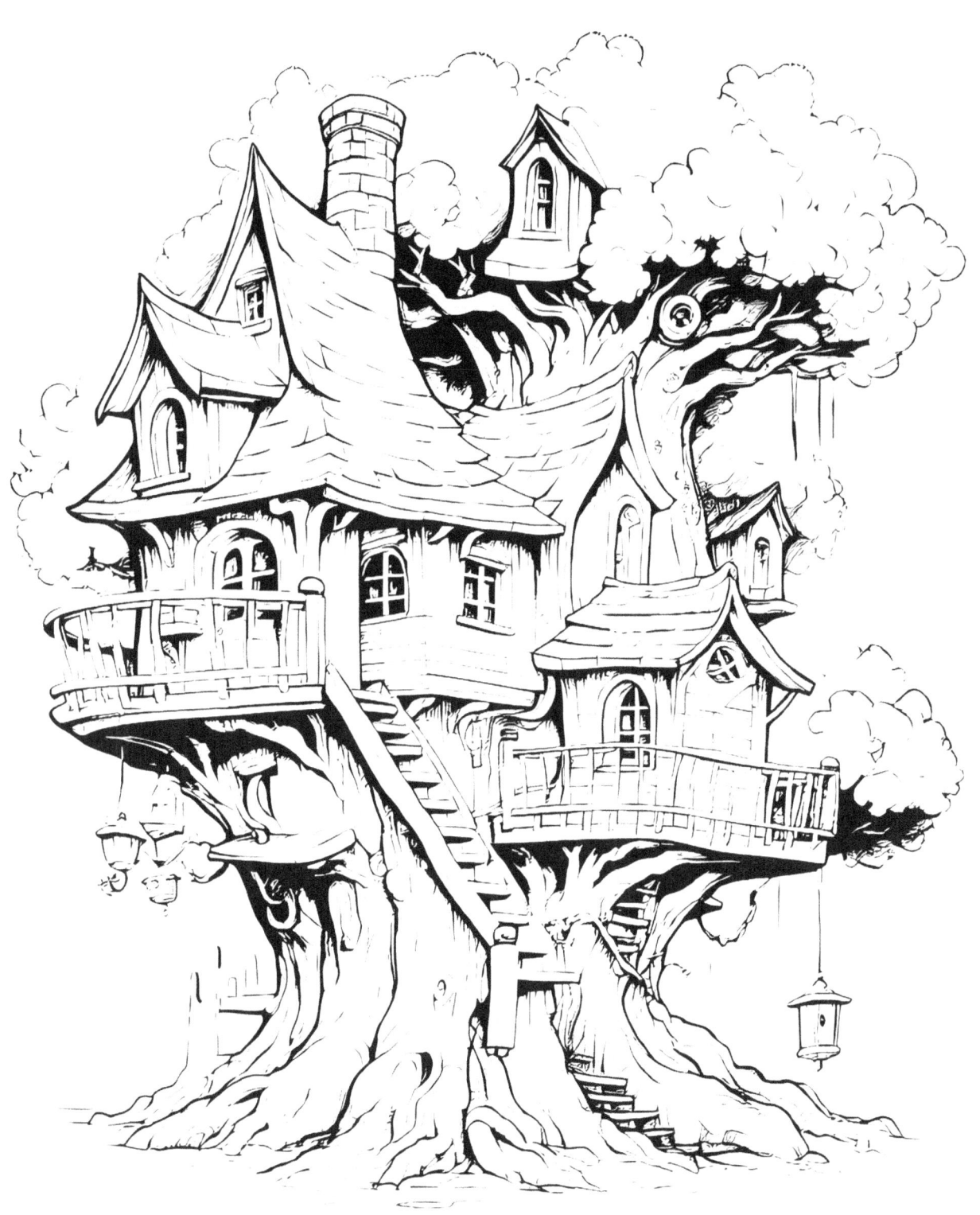

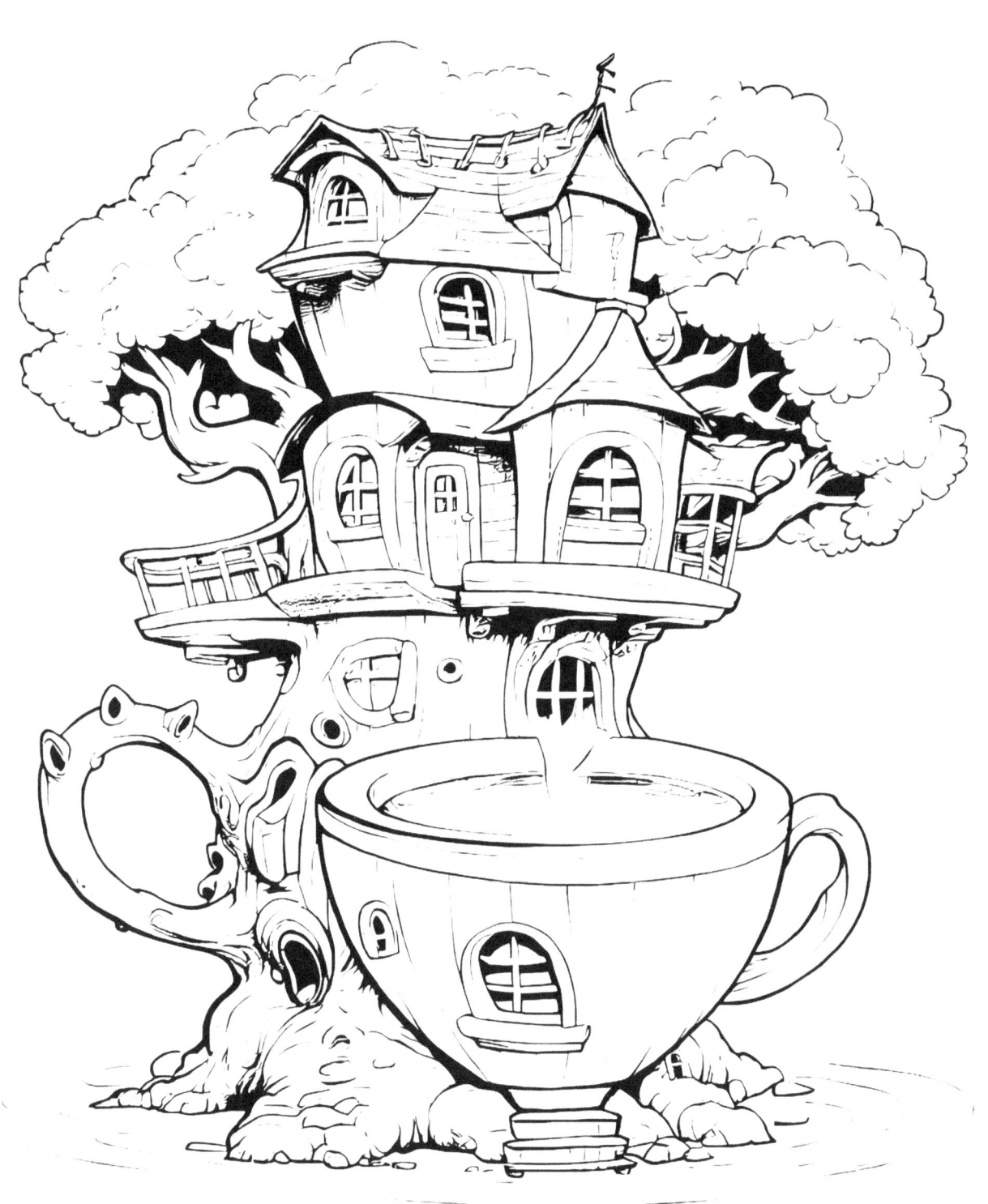

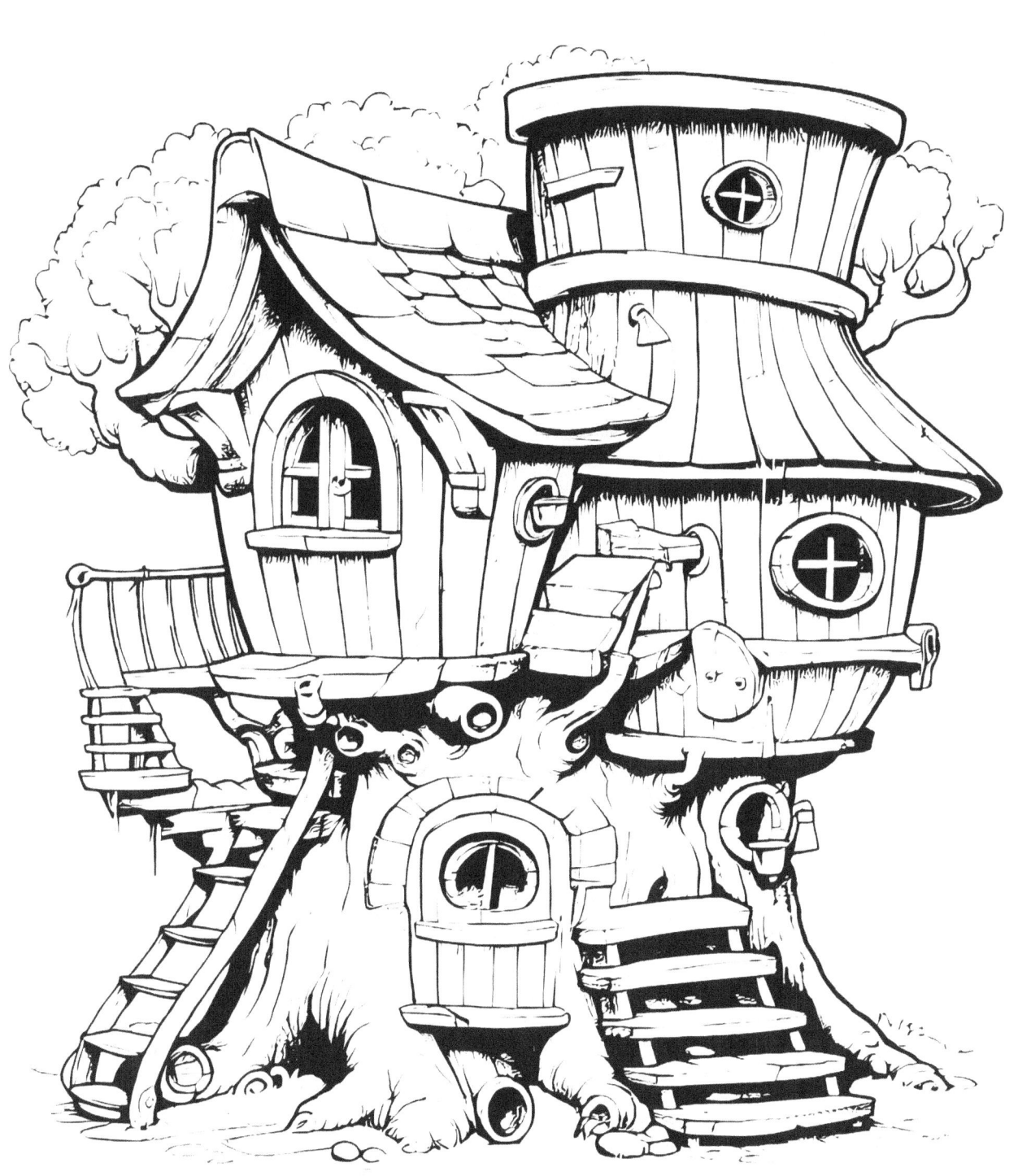

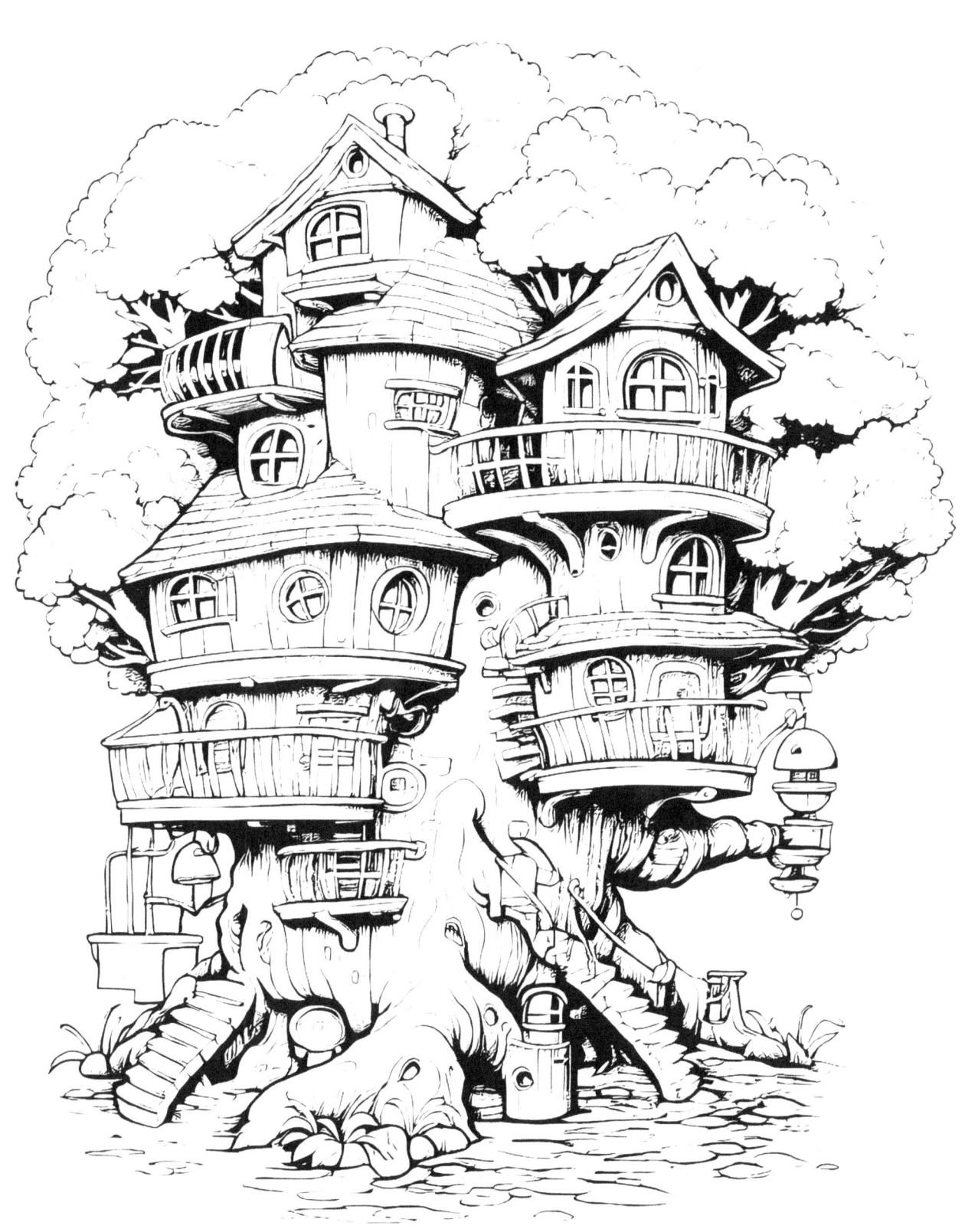

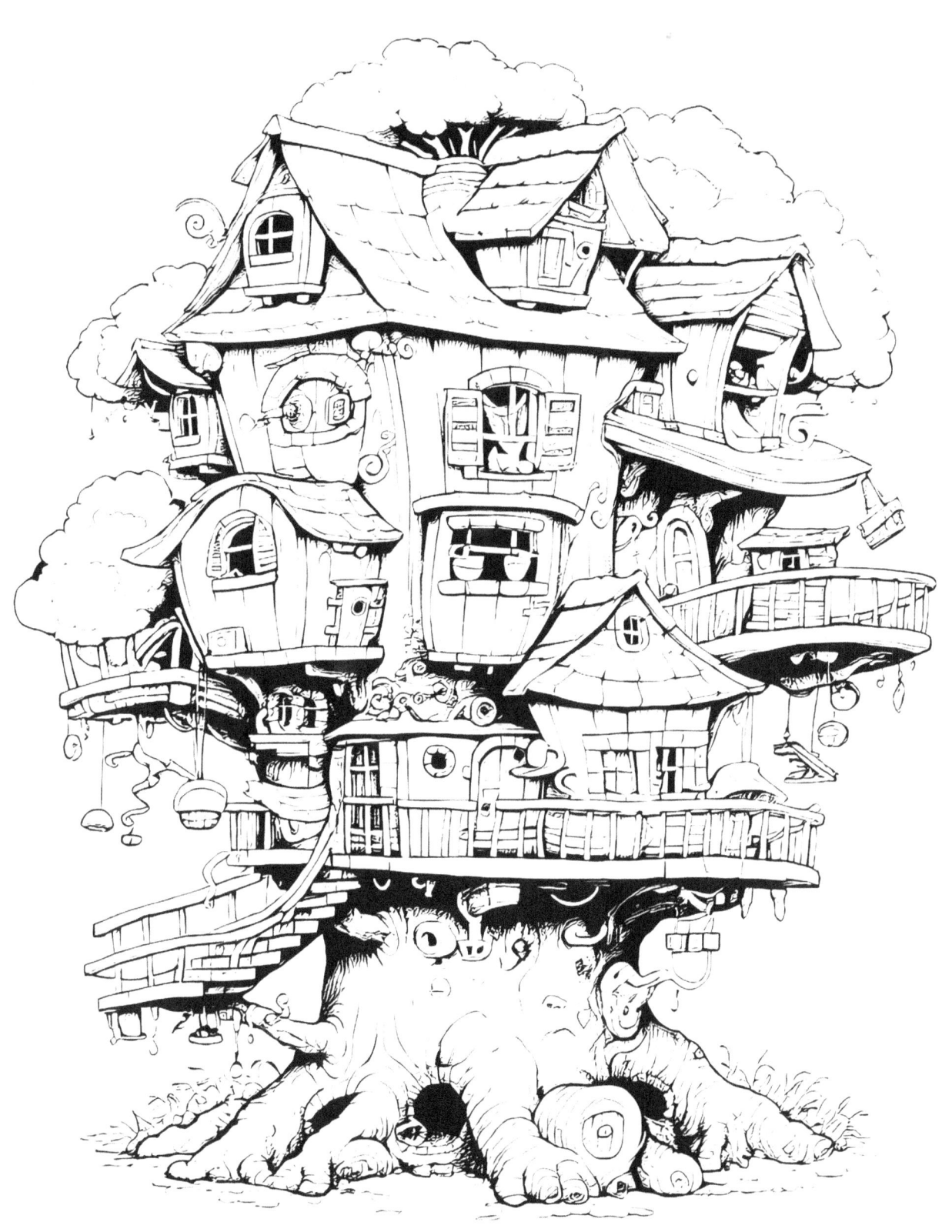

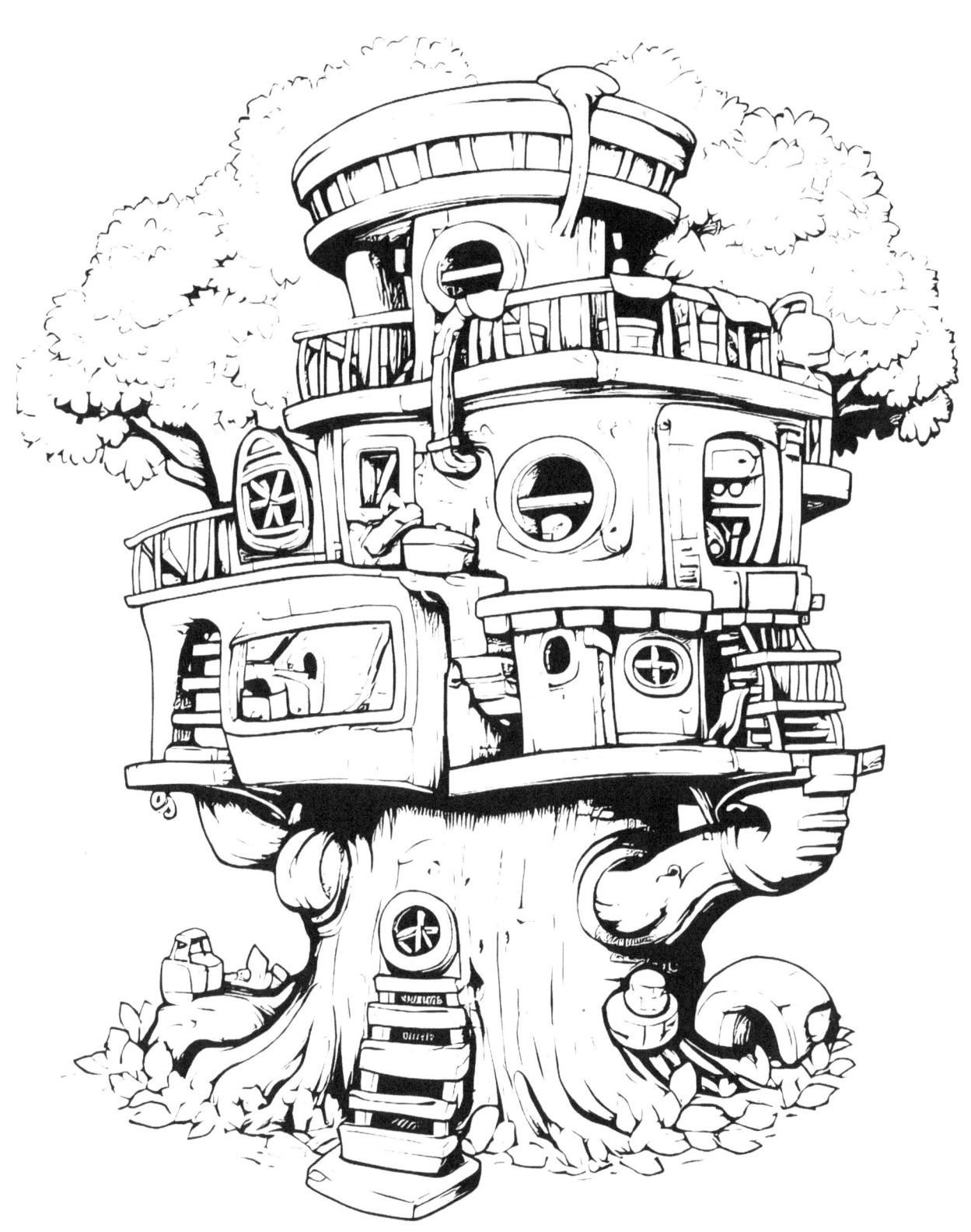

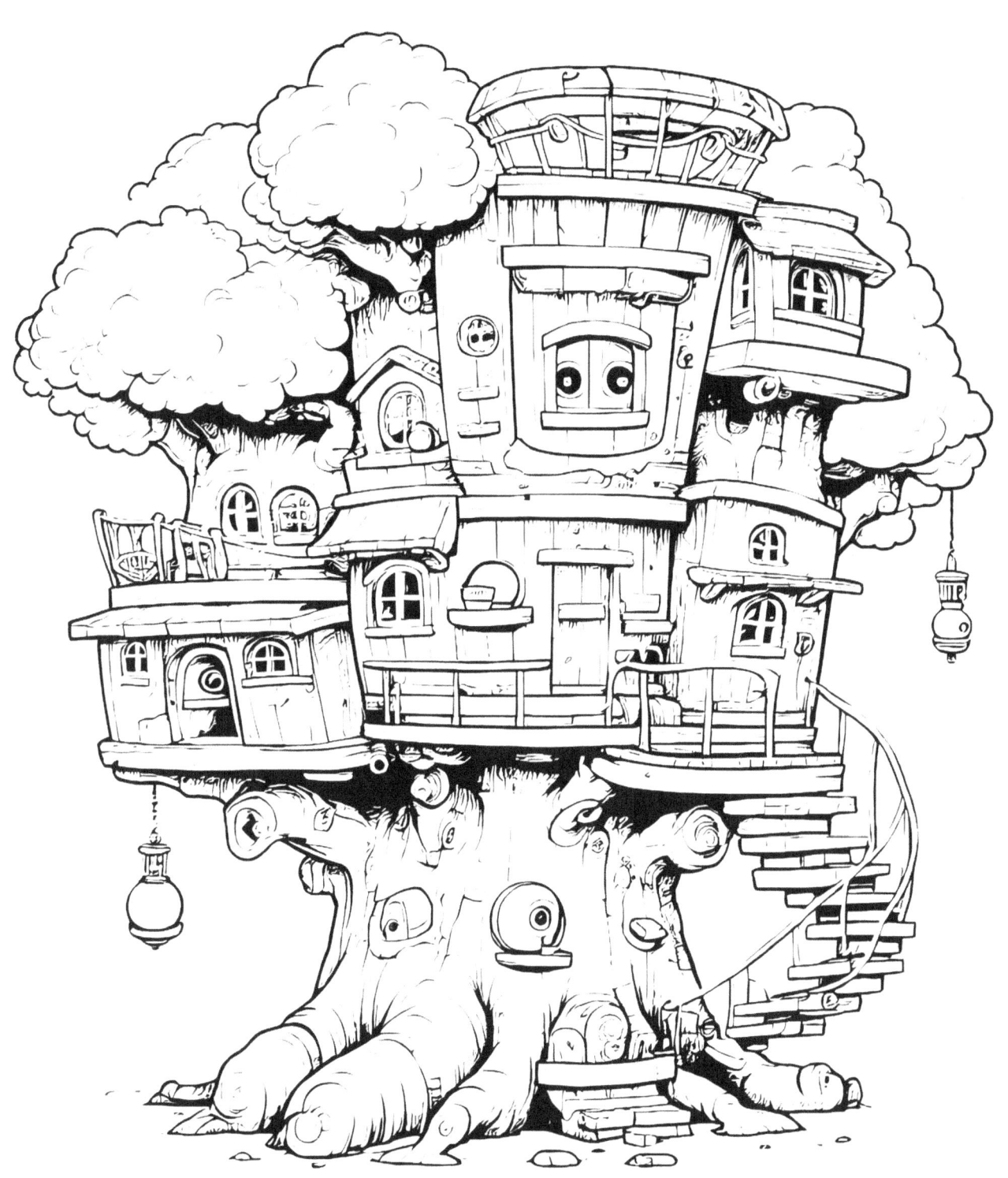

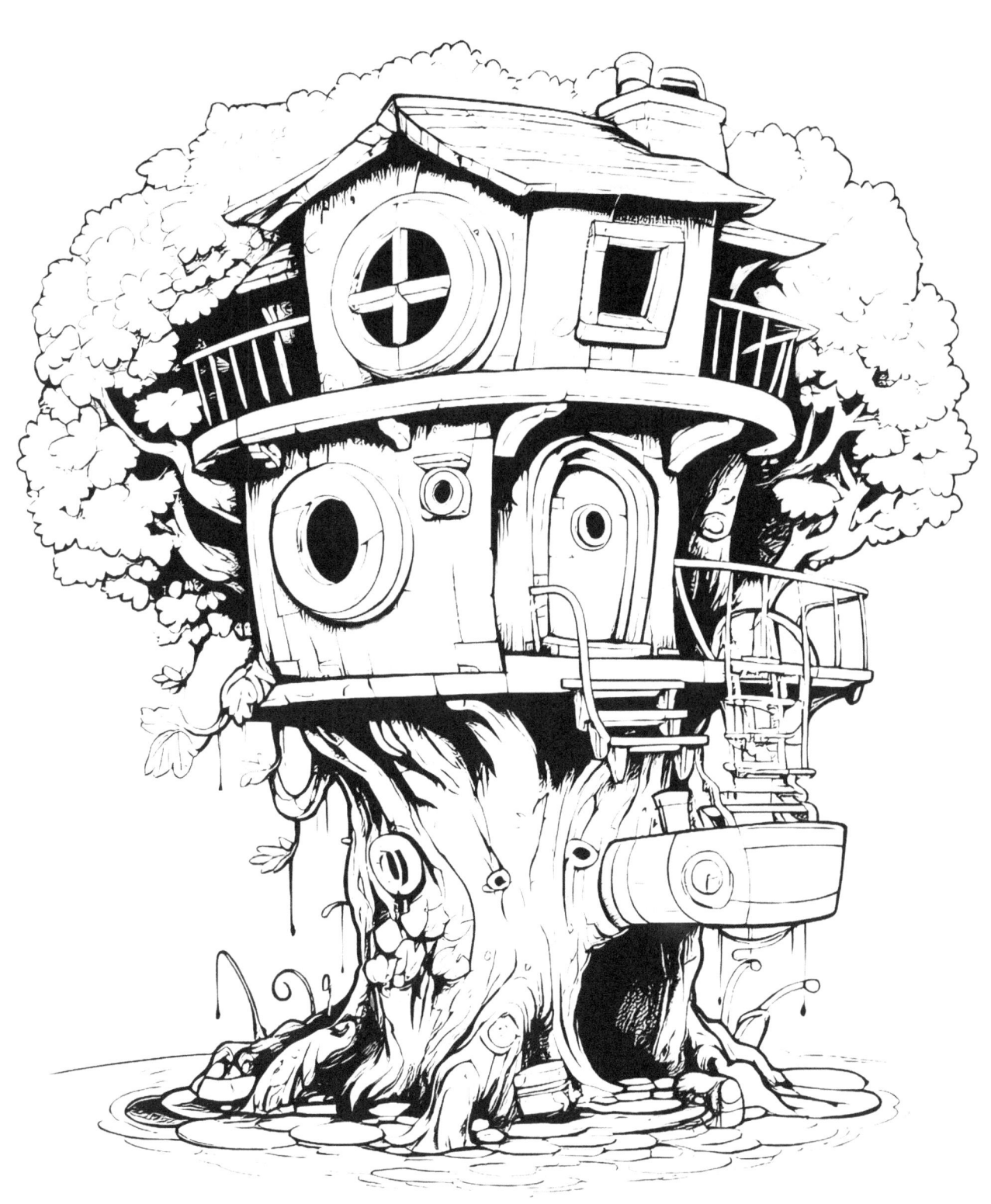

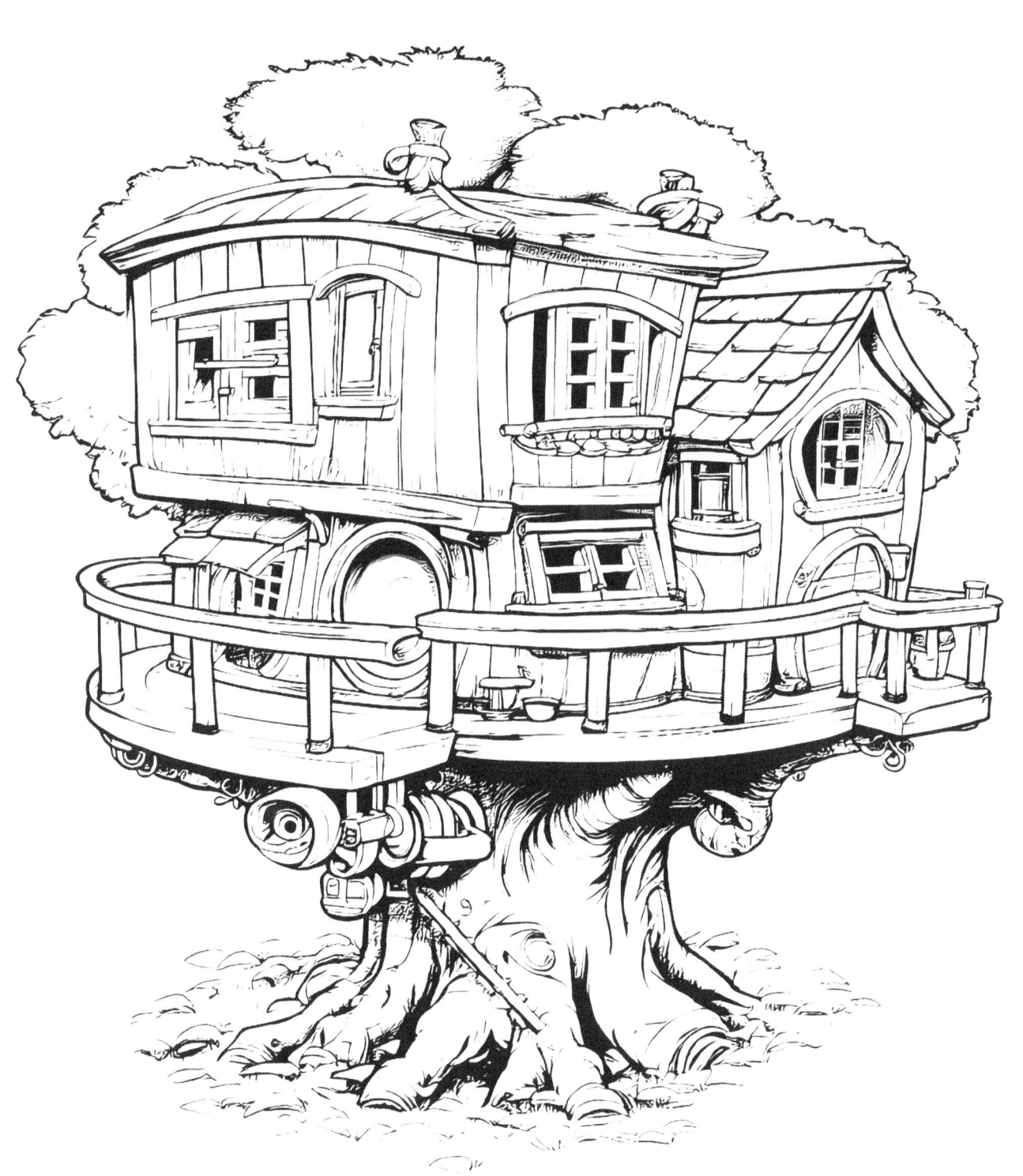

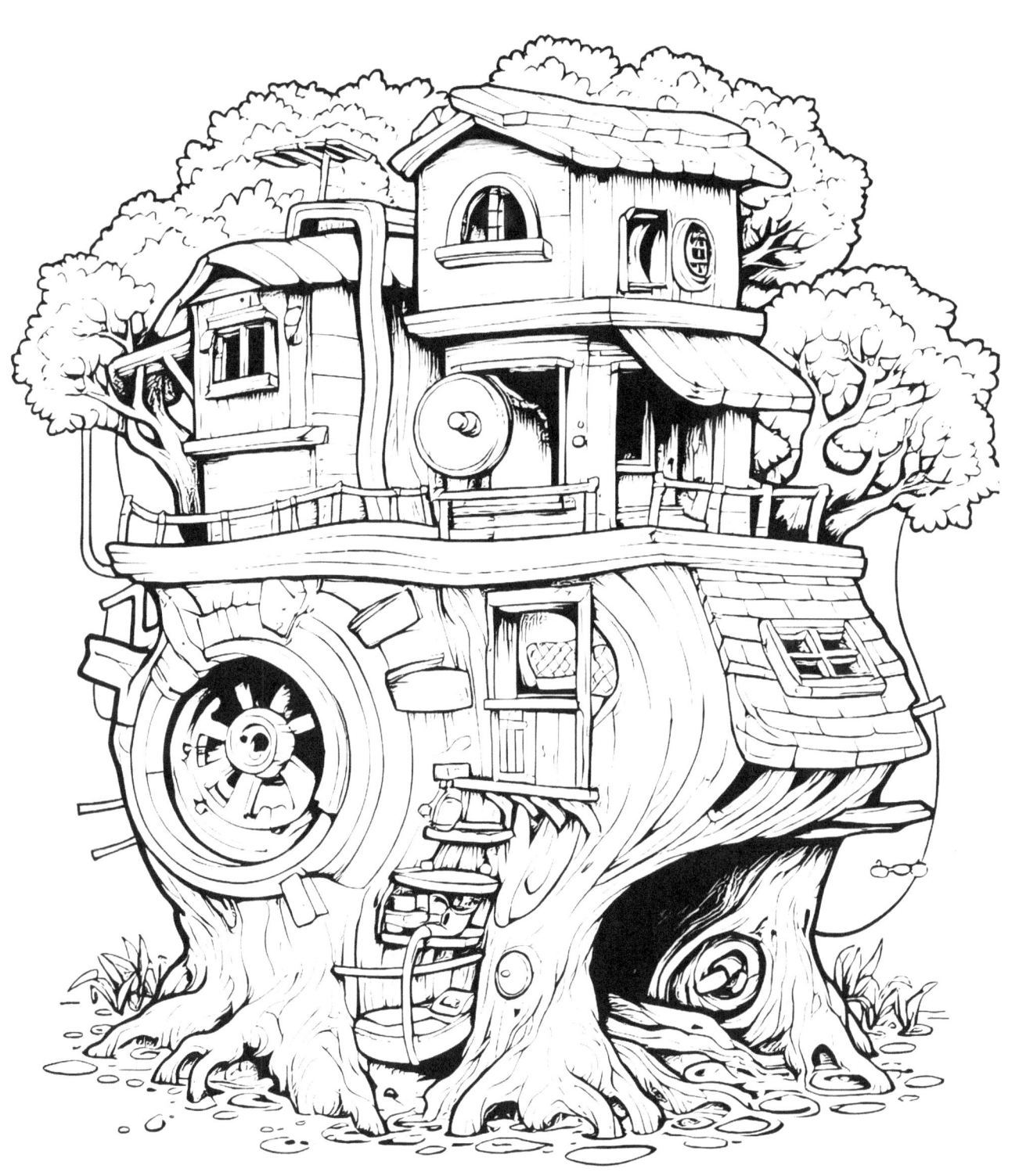

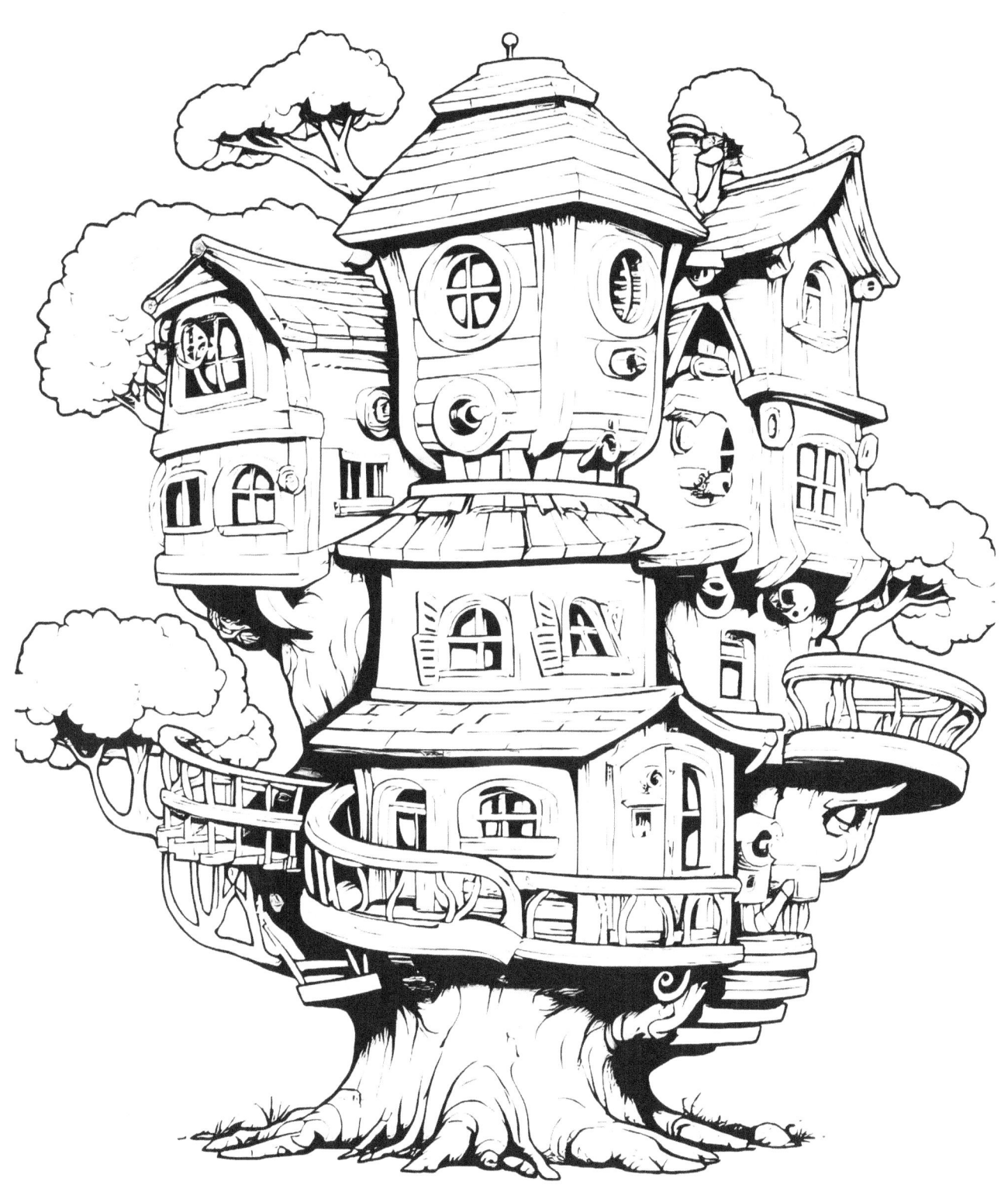

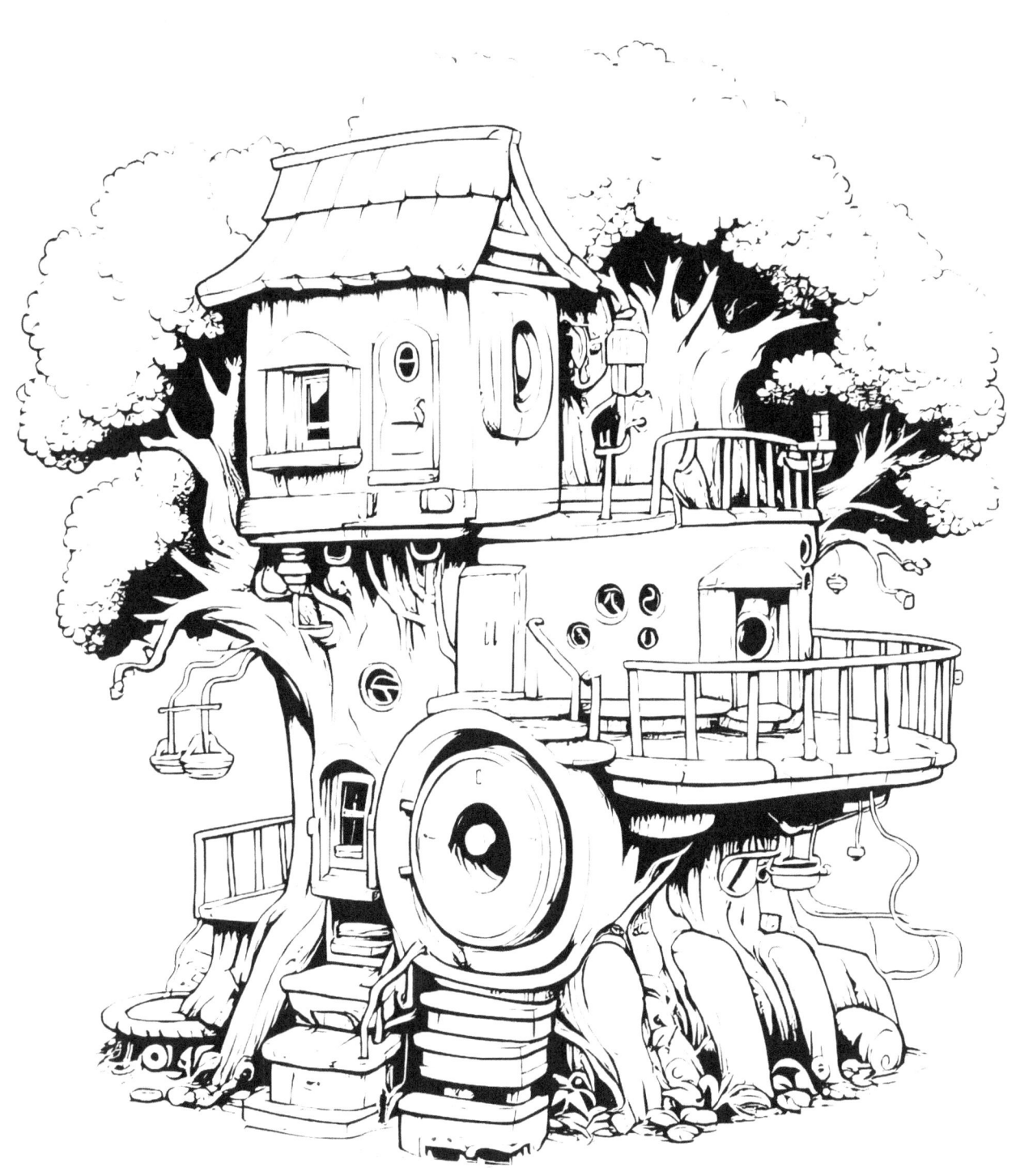

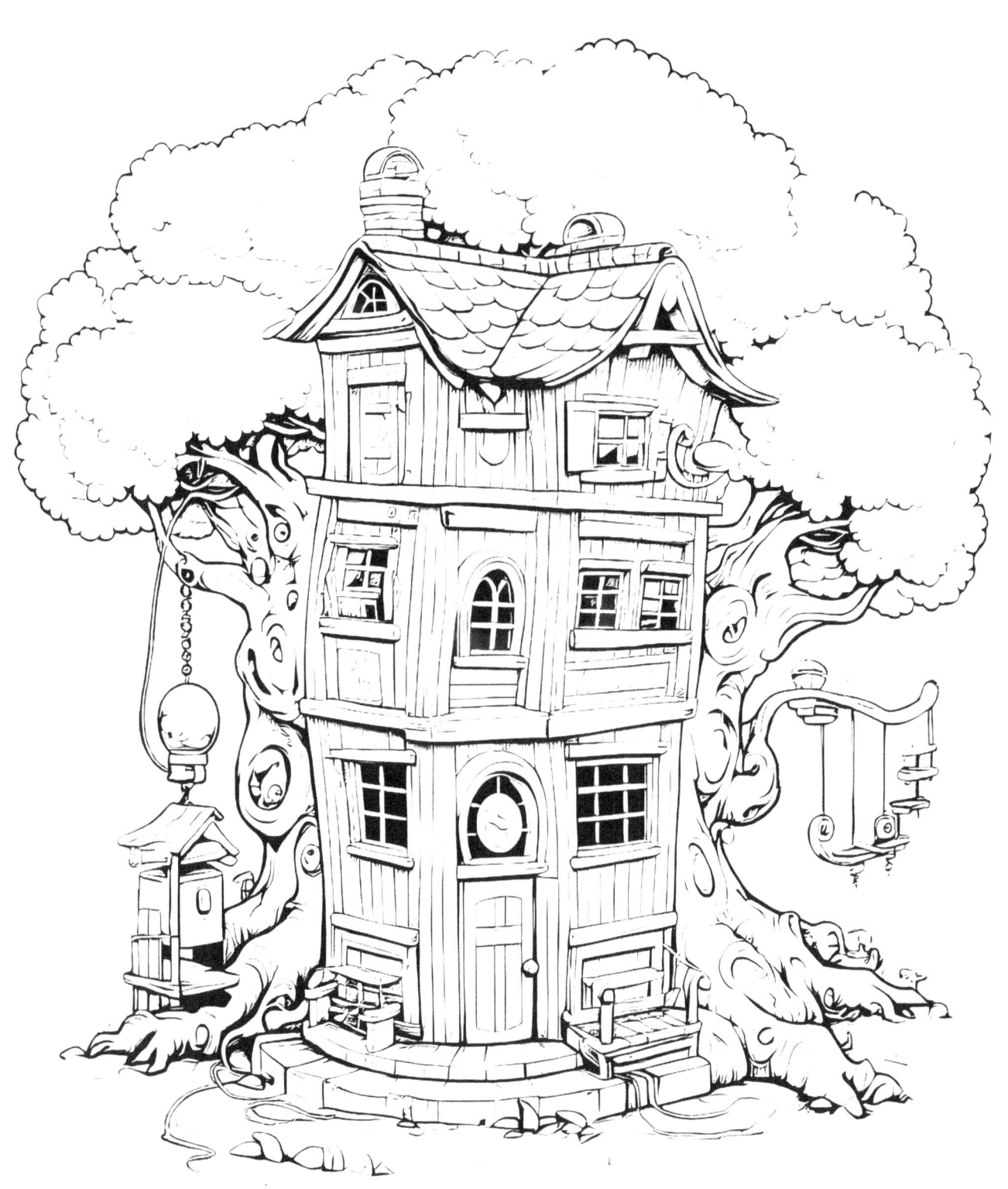

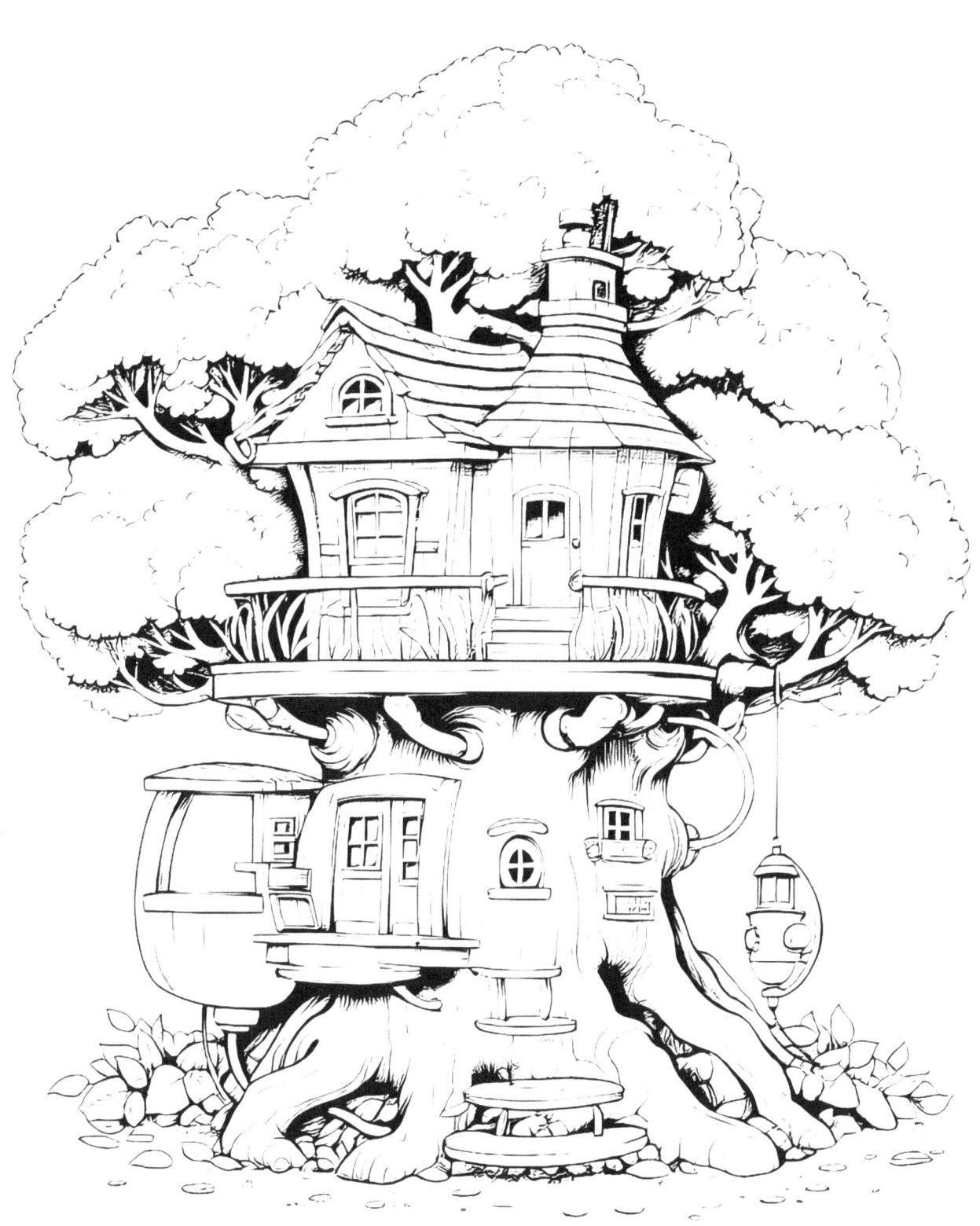

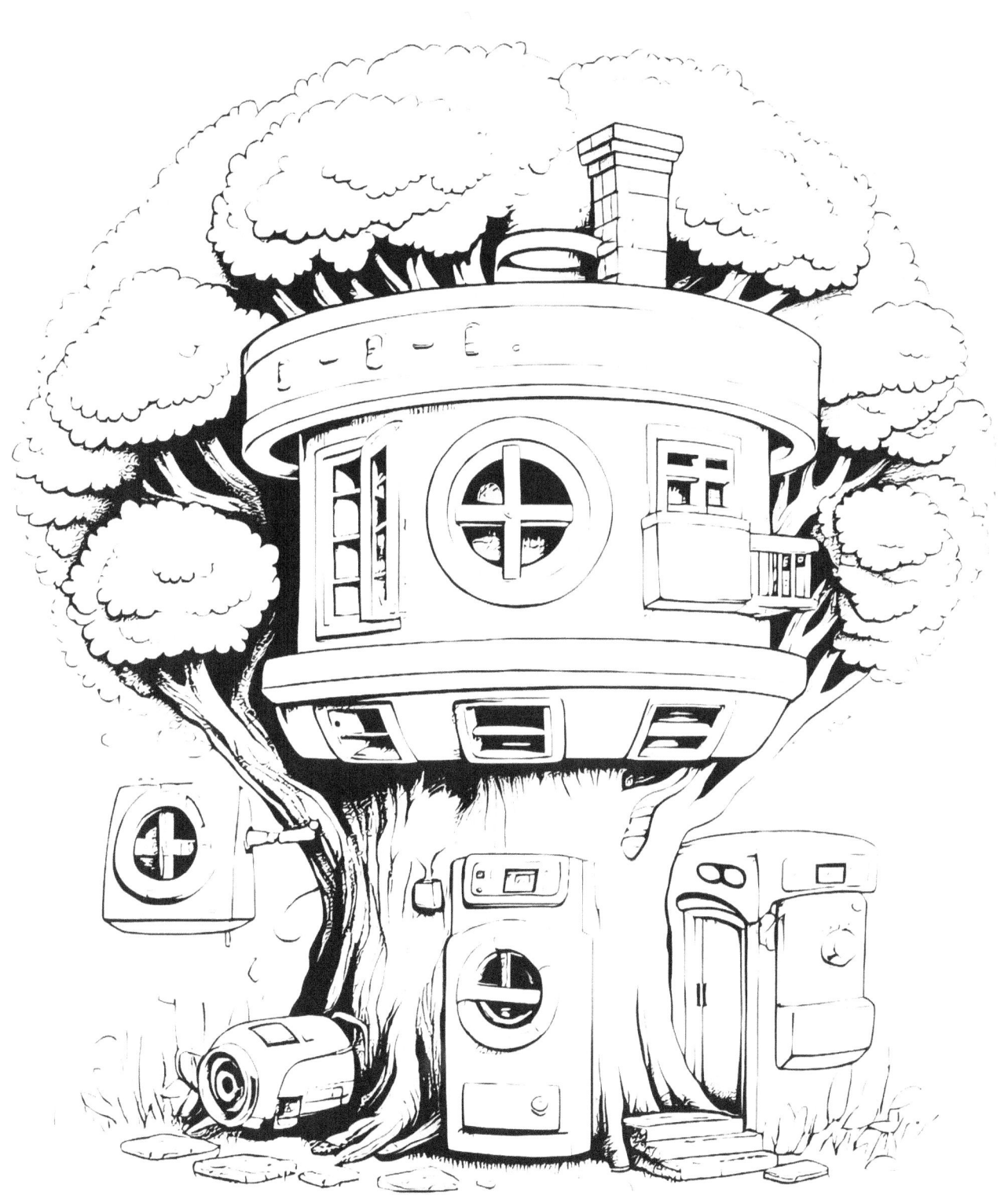

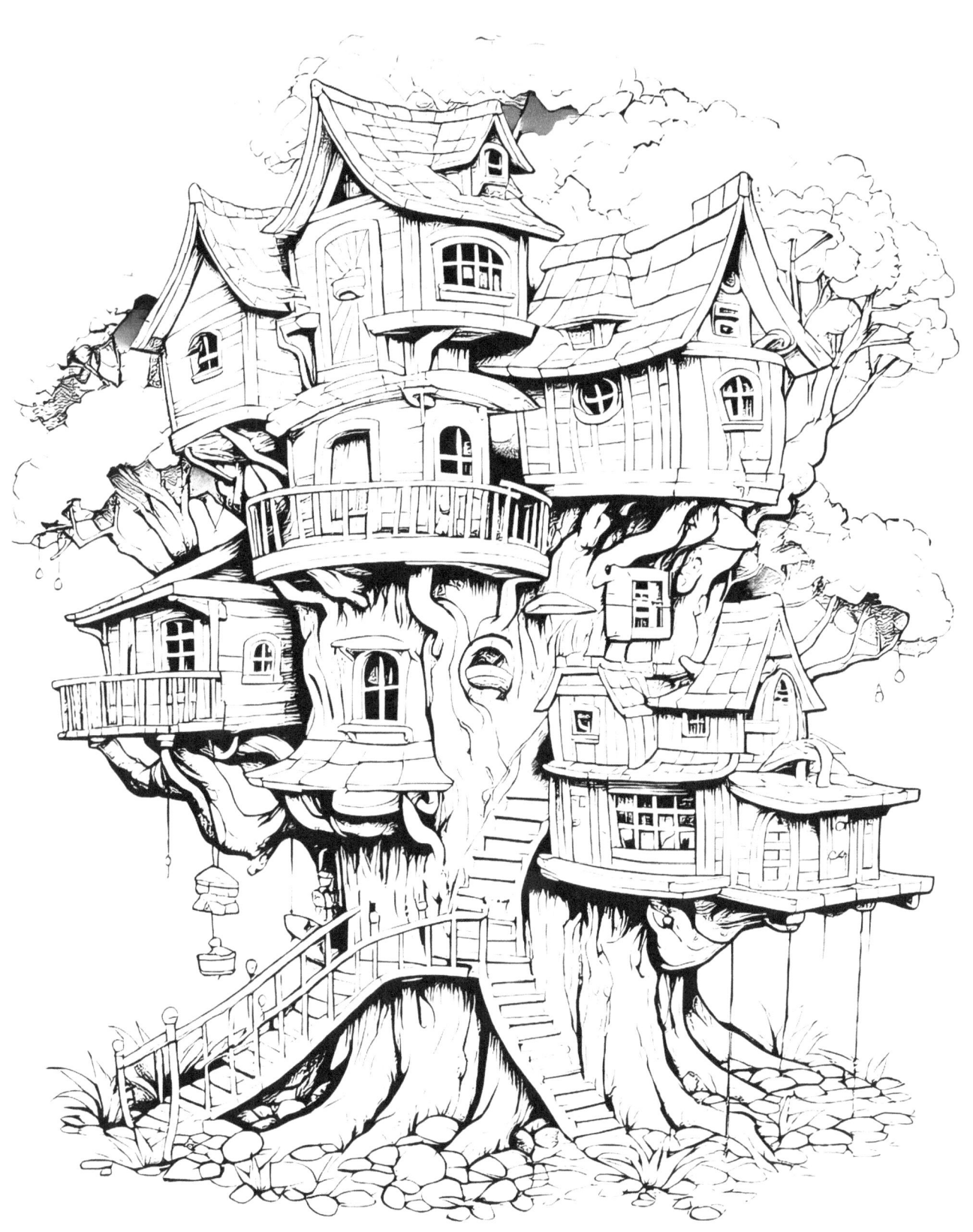

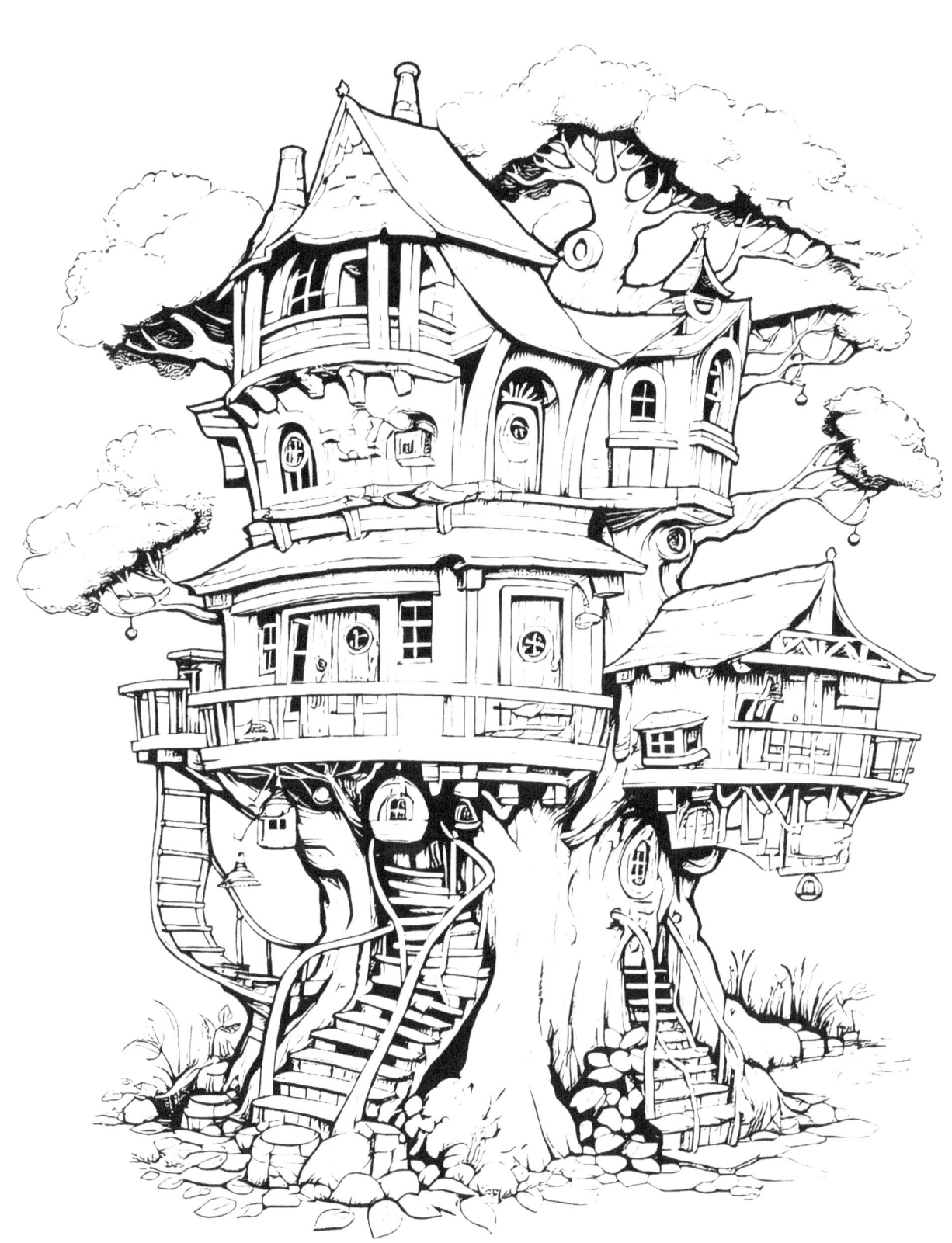

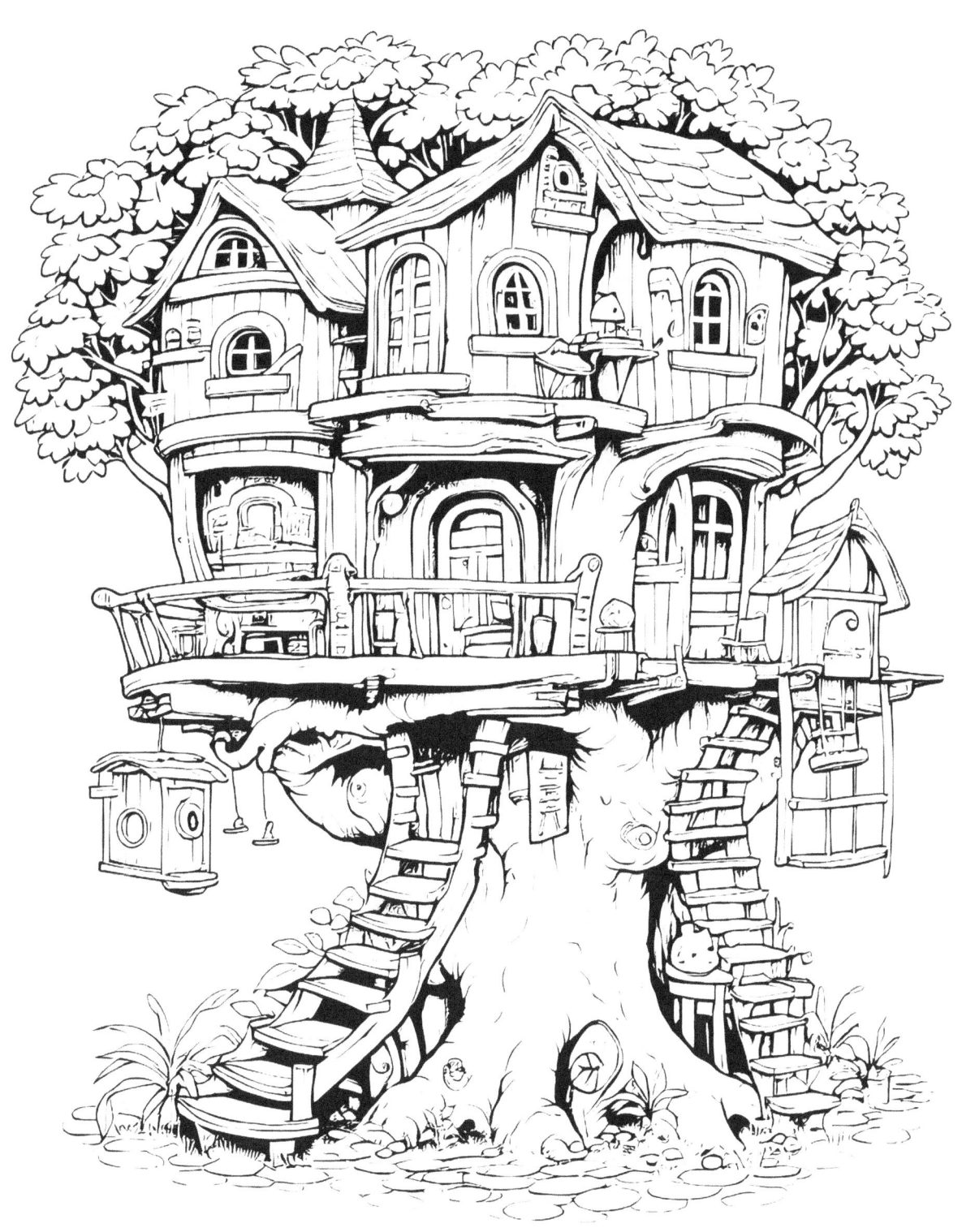